*Musar for Moderns*

# Musar for Moderns

BY

## Rav Elyakim Krumbein

KTAV, Jersey City, NJ
and Yeshivat Har Etzion, Alon Shevut, Israel

Copyright © 2005 Yeshivat Har Etzion

Library of Congress Cataloging-in-Publication Data

Krumbain, Elyakim.
 Musar for moderns / by Elyakim Krumbein.
  p. cm.
 ISBN 0-88125-875-X
 1. Musar movement. 2. Jewish ethics. 3. Self-actualization – Religious
aspects – Judaism. 4. Spiritual life – Judaism. I. Title.
BJ1285.5.M8K78 2005
296.3'6 – dc22

2004031077


*Published by*

**KTAV Publishing House, Inc.**
930 Newark Avenue
Jersey City, NJ 07306
bernie@ktav.com
www.ktav.com
Tel. (201) 963-9524
Fax. (201) 963-0102

**Yeshivat Har Etzion**
Alon Shevut 90433, Israel
Tel. 972-2-993-7300
(212) 732-4874 (NY)
office@etzion.org.il
www.haretzion.org
www.vbm-torah.org

Typeset in Minion by Jerusalem Typesetting, www.jerusalemtype.com

Cover Design by Rebecca Poch
Cover Photography by Peter Hellebrand *&* Carlos Paes
*Oleh!* Marketing Communications *&* Design, info@oleh.com, www.oleh.com

# Acknowledgments

I would like to express my gratitude and indebtedness to all those who made this volume possible, though a few brief words will not do them justice. Pervading the subject matter are the images and examples of my life-teachers: my beloved and illustrious parents, Aaron and Judith Krumbein; and my great, revered rebbeim, Rav Yehuda Amital *shlita* and Rav Aharon Lichtenstein *shlita*. Their wisdom and ability created the extraordinary family-Torah environment in which I have been privileged to live and learn. May Hashem bless them all with many more productive years.

I acknowledge – without mentioning by name – my colleagues at Yeshivat Har Etzion, on both the educational staff and the administration. From their greatness of character, individually and collectively, I haven't learned enough.

My thanks to Rabbi Reuven Ziegler, for his encouragement and assistance in the production of *Musar for Moderns* from its inception.

My dear wife Sarah reviewed almost all the material. Special thanks are due to her for her invaluable support as well as her specific suggestions.

Without the help and inspiration of many others – teachers, friends, family members and talmidim – the book would not be what it is. I beg their forgiveness for not mentioning all by name. May Hashem reward them.

I am glad to extend my gratitude to the following people who permitted the use of the citations in the book:

Dr. Tovah Lichtenstein, for the quotations from *Lonely Man of Faith* and *Worship of the Heart*, by Rabbi Joseph B. Soloveitchik; Dr. Daniel Shalit, for permission to quote from his book *Sichot Penim*; Dr. Haym Soloveitchik, for the quotations from *Ish Ha-Halakhah* and *Majesty and Humility*, by Rabbi Joseph B. Soloveitchik.

Musar for Moderns is based on a series which appeared originally on the website of Yeshivat Har Etzion's Israel Koschitzky Virtual Beit Midrash, www.vbm-torah.org.

Elyakim Krumbein
Tevet 5765

# Contents

Acknowledgments . . . . . . . . . . . . . . . . . . . . . . . . . . . . . . . . . . . . . . . . . v

Author's Foreword . . . . . . . . . . . . . . . . . . . . . . . . . . . . . . . . . . . . . . . . ix

Shiur 1:   There Must Be a Way. . . . . . . . . . . . . . . . . . . . . . . . . . .1

Shiur 2:   *Olam Ha-Zeh, Olam Ha-Ba –*
           This World and the Next (PART I) . . . . . . . . . . . . . . . 9

Shiur 3:   *Olam Ha-Zeh, Olam Ha-Ba –*
           This World and the Next (PART II) . . . . . . . . . . . . . .17

Shiur 4:   *Anava* (Humility) (PART I). . . . . . . . . . . . . . . . . . . . 25

Shiur 5:   *Anava* (Humility) (PART II) . . . . . . . . . . . . . . . . . . .33

Shiur 6:   Musar and 'Normality' (PART I). . . . . . . . . . . . . . . .41

Shiur 7:   Musar and 'Normality' (PART II) . . . . . . . . . . . . . . .53

Shiur 8:   Musar and 'Normality' (PART III). . . . . . . . . . . . . . 59

Shiur 9:   The Dynamics of Growth (PART I) . . . . . . . . . . . . . 67

Shiur 10:  Dynamics of Growth (PART II) . . . . . . . . . . . . . . . . 75

Shiur 11:  Rav Yisrael Salanter's Technique (PART I) . . . . . . . . . . 83

Shiur 12:  Rav Yisrael Salanter's Technique (PART II) . . . . . . . . . 93

Shiur 13:  The Depth of Mind . . . . . . . . . . . . . . . . . . . . . . . . .101

Shiur 14:  Ethical Ascent Through Prayer (PART I) . . . . . . . . . . 109

Shiur 15:  Ethical Ascent Through Prayer (PART II) . . . . . . . . . .119

Shiur 16:  Cognition . . . . . . . . . . . . . . . . . . . . . . . . . . . . . . . . .125

Shiur 17:  Summing Up – and Taking It From Here. . . . . . . . . . .139

Index . . . . . . . . . . . . . . . . . . . . . . . . . . . . . . . . . . . . . . . . . . . . . .145

# Author's Foreword

Our rabbis expressed the view that teachers of Torah ought to be as impeccable as angels. Hence my feeling of ethical ambivalence, as I send this book to press. Although I do teach Torah on a daily basis, this educational effort in particular gives me pause for reflection. For here I am trying to reach out to a larger audience, and help people find their bearings in an area of crucial personal importance. The implied presumptuousness becomes more open to question, and sobering thoughts about one's worthiness for the task are aroused. Such probing is of course a private affair. Suffice it to say here that I find it necessary to briefly address this assumption of responsibility.

If we examine precedents for this dilemma, it becomes clear that by and large, the tradition opposes that passivity which is the child of self-doubt. Self-doubt has its merits to be sure, but its power to paralyze is not among them. The classic exemplar, the author of *Chovot Ha-Levavot*, arrived at this conclusion for himself.[1] He decided that one question is paramount: is there a need? If the answer is affirmative, then "try to be a man where there are no men". This book responds to what I perceive as a need.

In the past, a tone of openness and general humanity has often accompanied the study and practice of Musar. In fact, we find that this attitude was deemed essential. For example: Lithuanian Musar masters revived awareness of man's innate intelligence as a source of moral imperative, thus concluding that a vast proportion of Torah obligations applies not only to Jews. "Man is obligated to fulfill anything that intelligence dictates, and to be wary of transgressing it, even if not commanded by God…When God created man He gave him the power of wisdom, designed to be used as a means of discovering the path that he should tread and how to conduct himself. He was created with his own natural *sefer Torah*…"[2] Yet in our time, this aspect frequently appears to be ignored and little known. Personal progress in the ethical sphere tends to be conceived in terms of another strain which can be found within our sources – one characterized by sternness, severity, withdrawal from the world "out there" and from its temptations. Without denying the intrinsic merits of the approach, this image effectively removes a sphere of religious interest from the purview of many who may need it the most. This is the state of affairs that I would like to address.

These proffered *shiurim* try to open a doorway. They recognize that the modern Jew, replete with all the freedoms and conflicts of modern man, needs to be re-licensed as the guardian of his own spiritual life. The *mesorah*, viable, vital and timeless, is the only possible source for such a license. It is a license that implies privilege, but in keeping with our tradition, it consists primarily of great responsibility.

The ideas herein are themselves the result of extended searching, developed with the aid of participants in oral and Internet *shiurim*. In presenting them to the larger public, I hope that as in the past, they will encourage and guide others in engaging a similar search. If they inspire further writing and publication by those more qualified than I to deal with this concern, I will be doubly satisfied.

## Notes

1. We will have occasion to examine this source later on (infra, shiur 5).
2. Rav Avraham Grodzinsky ל"ז, Torat Avraham, Bnei Berak 5738, p. 258. The concept is developed there at length. See also Dov Katz, T'nuat ha-Musar, Tel Aviv 1954, vol. 2. pp. 193–194, and Dr. Norman Lamm, Torah u-Madda, Jerusalem 5757, pp. 31–32, in connection with the curriculum at Kelm.

# Shiur one

# There Must Be a Way

In this first *shiur*, I will outline what we will be doing in the future. Before anything else, I think I should define what I mean by Musar. I will use this term in a broad sense that will be best understood by contrasting it with two other major areas of Torah study: *Halakha* and *Machshava*. *Halakha* teaches the Torah-committed Jew how to act, usually in a given situation. *Machshava*, Jewish thought, develops his world-outlook. But whenever one is engaging in study whose avowed aim is to learn how to live, how to *be*, one is studying Musar. The Kotzker Rebbe once put it succinctly to a certain *talmid chakham*: 'You learn so much Torah, but tell me, what have you learned from the Torah?' This definition may not be clear now, but I hope that the ensuing discussion will help sharpen matters.

I promised to describe our program, but I request your further indulgence. Before we talk about what we'll be doing, we must talk about why we'll be doing it. As is well known, the 'why' of Musar as an independent endeavor is, and always has been, controversial. Those who think Musar superfluous can certainly summon several *gedolei Yisrael* to support their view. I'm not out to change their minds, and I presume they aren't going to read this book. However, in order to grasp where we are going, I feel that I must state the opposing view on this question, which is really the assumption on which these *shiurim* are based.

Ostensibly, the critics are right. In order to live a Torah life, one must know what the Halakha demands. One needs also to understand why one must adhere to the mitzvot, for understanding is the basis of commitment and fulfillment. These matters are addressed fully by the vast literature of Halakha and Machshava. Dealing with these two areas alone is already a prodigious undertaking. Why devote precious time to anything else?

The answer is that living a Torah-committed life is a much more complex challenge than the critics would have us believe. How to live is a question that needs to be dealt with directly. It is not something that can be sufficiently known or sensed, automatically or intuitively, by studying how to behave in given circumstances or by probing the nature of existence.

I will presently demonstrate this claim, at the same time foreshadowing a technique that I will use continuously: quotation of sources, intended for the reader's careful study and attention. The progress of the *shiurim* will, as a rule, take for granted such study on the part of the reader.

There are whole worlds of Torah fulfillment that are wont to be ignored by those who would restrict their attention to the Law and its philosophical foundations. The first example we will survey can be inferred from the Ramban's well-known comment on *Kedoshim tihyu* ('You shall be holy,' Vayikra 19:2):

> The point is that the Torah prohibits incest and forbidden foods, while permitting marital relations and consumption of food and wine. It follows that a hedonist could find legitimacy for depravity with his wife or with many wives, excessively indulge in wine and meat, and utter foul language without restraint, for this has not been expressly forbidden in the Torah. As a result, he would be a scoundrel licensed by the Torah.

There are examples of immoral behavior that are not to be found spelled out in Halakha. A student of Halakha alone could conceivably be a scoundrel. In order to avoid this, the Torah had to stipulate that there is a general mitzva of *kedusha* (holiness), which is not halakhically defined, and which sets no uniform standards. As Ramban continues:

> Therefore, Scripture, after specifying the things which are absolutely forbidden, admonishes in a general way that we should abstain from excesses: diminishing marital relations, as the Rabbis said, 'So that *talmidei chakhamim* not be with their wives constantly like roosters,' and sanctifying oneself by minimizing wine-drinking, as the nazirite is called 'holy' …and guarding one's mouth and tongue from contamination through excessive eating and foul speech …so sanctifying oneself until attainment of the level of abstinence ascribed to Rabbi Hiyya, of whom it was said that he never in his life uttered an idle word.

The letter of the law has a spirit behind it, which points us toward the larger goal of the Torah: striving for perfection, which can be mandated only in general terms, and which allows for varying levels of achievement in accordance with individual characteristics. Neglecting this responsibility leads to the phenomenon of the 'scoundrel licensed by the Torah' – immorality that violates no formal statute.

The second area that is apt to be sacrificed by single-minded attention to the Law is a realm that the Law refers to, when at all, with great brevity and generality: the realm of personality and emotions. There are in the Torah 'commanded emotions,' such as love and fear of God, love of one's fellow, and so on. But, as opposed to commanded action, commanded emotion is not something that can be put into effect in any immediate or obvious way. If love is not there to begin with, how can one put it there? How does one rid oneself of negative traits? There is a common conception that preoccupation with Torah study is, in itself, a remedy, if not a panacea. The divine light of Torah is said to possess the capacity for moral rectification. For those who rely on this theory, the Vilna Gaon has some bad tidings. Consider his explanation of the Torah's simile, 'Let my teaching fall like rain':[1]

> Rain falls everywhere and acts on everything equally. But its effect corresponds to the recipient. Where wheat is sown, the rain causes

wheat to grow. Where poisonous plants are sown, the rain will make them grow too. Yet the rain itself is always characterized as good. Thus, the Torah, which descends from Heaven, works its action to cause whatever is in a man's heart to grow. If his heart is good, the Torah will increase his fear of God. But if his heart contains a poison root, he will falter all the more when he studies Torah, and the evil in his heart will increase.

The idea propounded by the Gaon may strike us as odd. We will soon get an inkling of one way this can happen. In any event, the Law per se does not address this problem. Preoccupation with Torah, startlingly, can make things worse. A way has to be found to get at the root, to replace the poison seed with a healthy one.

Apart from types of corruption not specifically prohibited by Halakha, and apart from the problematics of *tikkun* (improvement) of the self, regarding which Halakha and Machshava offer little insight, there is a third area which demonstrates that the subject-matter of Musar can be ignored only at great spiritual peril. It appears that it is entirely possible for great students of Halakha, the most Torah-committed Jews, to be responsible for moral failures, even calamities. And this, not because of any laxity of purpose, but, on the contrary: as a direct result of their knowledge and commitment.

The Netziv, in the introduction to his Torah commentary *Ha'amek Davar*, writes that the verse 'Righteous and straight (*yashar*, usually translated 'honest') is He' refers to the reason for the destruction of the Second Temple.

> The Jews of the time were righteous and pious and toiled in the Torah, but they were not 'straight' in the ways of the world. As a result, because of the groundless hatred in their hearts, when they saw someone who acted contrary to their views on God-fearing behavior, they suspected him of being a Sadducee or a heretic. This eventually led to blood being spilled and every possible calamity, until the Temple was destroyed. And this Divine verdict is justified in the above-mentioned verse, for the Holy One is 'straight,' and does not tolerate such righteous men. He only favors righteous people

*4*

who are straight in the ways of the world, but not those who go in crooked paths, even if they do so for the sake of Heaven (*le-shem Shamayim*), for this causes the desolation of Creation and the destruction of civilization.

The Netziv describes righteous men whose vocation was to toil in Torah but had hatred in their hearts. Remember the principle taught by the Gaon. Here we have a historical illustration. These 'righteous people' would never knowingly have persecuted anyone out of sheer hatred or jealousy. They did it *le-shem Shamayim*, after determining that someone was a heretic. Unbeknownst to themselves, this verdict was motivated by hatred and jealousy. Their Torah was their undoing. Their proficiency in Torah polemics enabled them to prove conclusively that this person deserved the fate they assigned him. Their total commitment to Torah empowered their resolve to wipe out the evil they were convinced they saw. Yet this commitment served only as a mask, a means of rationalizing the subconscious directives of *sinat chinam*, groundless hatred.

Torah represents the highest ideal. Its peril lies in its very grandeur and power. Undistilled souls, who cleave to Torah with what they take for idealistic passion, are at risk. They may be flirting with perversion.

I would like, with some trepidation, to bring another source – a controversial one – related to this issue. *Em Ha-Banim Semecha* is a work written in Hungary in the throes of the Holocaust by an eminent rabbi, Rav Yissachar Teichtal, who became convinced that the opposition to Zionism on religious grounds had been a tragic error that helped seal the doom of countless Jews. In his book, he attempts to persuade his peers to support the rebuilding of *Eretz Yisrael*. In the following passage, he is resigned to his inevitable lack of success. The anti-Zionists had used the classic mold of halakhic argumentation to make their point, but Rav Teichtal presents his own analysis:

> Those who are biased to begin with will not see the truth and will not accept our words, and all the proof in the world will not help, for they are so smitten with blindness that self-interest will blind their

eyes, so that they deny even things that are as clear as day. For who today is greater than the scouts [sent by Moshe], whose worthiness is attested by Scripture? Yet, since considerations of office biased them (as is explained at length in the Zohar and the *Shelah*, for they feared that they would lose their posts as heads of the tribes), they therefore despised the desired Land, deluding others in their wake…. So it is in our time, even regarding rabbis, rebbes, and Hasidim. This one has a good rabbinic post, this one a good Hasidic court, and this one has a good business or a good factory or a good respectable position with a large income, so the fear looms over them: if they go to *Eretz Yisrael*, their situation may deteriorate…. People like this are so biased by the self-interest hidden deep within their hearts that they do not even recognize the self-interest speaking from within, as I have brought in the name of our holy master, the man of God, Rav Yishaya Muskat of Prague …that a person usually deludes himself into believing that his actions are for the sake of Heaven, whereas in actuality he is being driven by a deeply hidden self-interest…. Likewise, see *Divrei Chayim* on Chanuka, who wrote that a man sees only what he wants to see, and therefore one's power of decision and judgment of the truth is null when he is prejudiced in any way….[2]

And now, who takes responsibility for all the innocent blood shed in our times by our sinfulness? It seems to me that all those leaders who prevented Jews from joining the builders of *Eretz Yisrael* will be unable to wipe their hands and say: Our hands did not spill this blood![3]

Such a chilling accusation can be made only by a man in the circumstances that overtook Rav Teichtal, and of his stature. We who were spared the Holocaust can be no more than silent bystanders at this debate. At the same time, when reading this anguished excerpt, I find it difficult to escape the conclusion that it is at least possible that he was right.

I would like to sum up the discussion that was the main body of this lesson. We spoke of three major areas, not directly addressed by

Halakha or Machshava, that are at risk: immoral behavior not specifically prohibited, inner personal morality, and the pitfall of crimes done for the sake of Heaven. I won't further belabor this matter, but instead will get on with the question: Where does one go from here?

Many serious-minded people, convinced of its necessity, naturally turned to Musar study, only to be dismayed at the unexpected obstacles frustrating their progress. Before long, it becomes clear that basic conviction and motivation are not enough. The questions arise: Can intellectual study really bring about existential change? Can it impart not only knowledge and acumen, but wisdom? If it can, why doesn't it seem to be doing so? If it can't, then what else needs to be done?

The problems do not end there. Today's committed Jew, who lives daily in consonance with the modern temper, finds that temper at variance with the fundamental ideas of what he perceives as the traditional Musar orientation. Otherworldliness, guilt, and humility, among other concepts, seem to be out of step with modernity. Can we still read *Mesillat Yesharim* the way our forebears did two centuries ago? Can we aspire to live Torah in its profoundest sense while still being a part of the twenty-first century? The frustration and even despair of many well-intentioned people who have made the attempt seems to indicate that answer to these questions, if it exists, is not a simple matter.

These problems inspired the idea for these *shiurim*. Our working assumption will be that there is a way.

Each of the coming sessions will be devoted to a specific issue connected to the content or techniques of Musar. Our discussions will have a dual focus.

One focus will be on problems that erect barriers on the way to rectification of the self. Some of these are matters uniquely faced by modern religious man, and others present quandaries intrinsic to human nature as such.

Second, we will be looking for the underlying approaches, or inner orientations, that influence our ability to engage this area productively. By exploring a variety of sources, the hope is that the student will be aided to the point where his quest ceases to be a blind groping, and becomes a search, guided and directed from within.

One final note. It should be clear from what I have said that we will not actually be 'doing' Musar. That is a daily affair and, if it is to have any meaning, cannot be done only periodically. If we succeed in removing some of the obstacles, and thereby make the search possible, we will have gained our objective. For modern man, this is no small achievement.

## Notes
1. From the Gaon's commentary to Mishle chap. 19, 9.
2. Em Ha-Banim Semecha, Jerusalem 1983, second introduction, p. 36.
3. Ibid. Haskamot (approbations), p. 18.

# Shiur two

# *Olam Ha-Zeh, Olam Ha-Ba* – This World and the Next

## PART I

THE FIRST TOPIC we will explore is one that I think most people take for granted and therefore do not trouble themselves to scrutinize seriously. This notwithstanding, the fact is that our attitude on this issue can have considerable impact on our efforts to live according to the Torah, certainly from the vantage point of Musar.

For many, this issue is also linked to one of the major hindrances to Musar study – namely, depression. Musar is often associated with melancholy; it is seen as engendering a psychological malaise that is ultimately counterproductive to the effort invested.

Consider the following excerpt from *Mesilat Yesharim* (chap. 1). Bear in mind that as a Musar work, *Mesilat Yesharim* will not achieve its aim if it is merely understood; it must be accepted. As you read, ask yourself, Do I identify with this? Moreover, *can* I identify? Do I *want* to?[1]

> Man was created solely in order to delight in God and derive pleasure from the glory of His Presence, which is the truest delight and the greatest possible pleasure. And the place of this pleasure is truly the World-to-Come, for it was created with that very design. But the

way to arrive at this, our desired destination, is the Present World, as our Rabbis of blessed memory said: 'This world is like a corridor to the next.' The means that bring a person to this end are the mitzvot commanded to us by God. And the only place where mitzvot may be fulfilled is the Present World.... Now the Holy One has put man in a place where there are many forces that can distance him from God. Such are those very physical lusts which, if he should tend after them, he would be removing himself continuously from the absolute good. It follows that man is really in the midst of a great battle, for all the events of the world, for better or for worse, are moral trials (*nisyonot*): poverty on the one hand, and wealth on the other, as Shlomo said (Proverbs 30): 'Lest I grow satisfied, for then I might deny, saying, 'Who is God?' And lest I become impoverished, for then I might steal.' Thus, the prospects of contentment, on the one hand, and suffering, on the other, mean that the battle is upon man, from the front as well as from the rear.

In essence, these sentiments can traced to *Kohelet*, who was disillusioned by the world and proclaimed it 'vanity of vanities.' Undoubtedly, there are readers who will wholeheartedly embrace this outlook.

Others may agree in principle with this view, but after introspection will be chagrined to find a lack of inner identification with it. This second group has been conditioned by modern life, even by modern religious life, to seek fulfillment in this world. The viewpoint that regards the world as a menacing existential minefield whose *raison d'etre* can be known only after death has been inimical to modern culture for over two hundred years. In effect, the *Mesilat Yesharim* is calling upon us to reject inwardly the messages that many of us find deeply ingrained in our psyches and inextricably woven into our upbringing. An awesome undertaking, no doubt.

But there is a third possible reaction to this passage. Rather than identify, or submit, there are those who will bridle. They do not view their positive involvement with the world and society as a necessary evil or as the result of massive conditioning, but as part of the way in which they would like to live their life. In essence, without meaning to be impertinent, they find themselves taking issue with the *Mesilat Yesharim*.

A member of the first group, beginning to study *Mesilat Yesharim* and encountering the passage quoted above, will encounter no more difficulty than a student living two hundred years ago. A member of the second group, in order to continue to grapple seriously with this work, would have to grit his teeth and prepare for rough going. As for the third group, would we fail to understand if they were to conclude that Musar is not for them?

At this point, I will introduce another excerpt, authored by an eminent halakhist who lived two generations ago, Rav Yechiel Yaakov Weinberg. It is taken from an article[2] in which he describes the aims and achievements of Rav Shimshon Raphael Hirsch, the rabbi who saved German Orthodoxy from desiccation during the Enlightenment. As you read, ask yourself how Rav Hirsch would view himself vis-à-vis the *Mesilat Yesharim*:

The Israelite religion does not wish to uproot the Jew from the soil of his growth and transplant him elsewhere. Rather, it wishes to influence the whole man, to prepare his whole heart, his thoughts and deeds, for his exalted tasks. All that is human is near to it, for Judaism is – as Rav Hirsch himself put it – flawless, perfected humanity, a Jewish humanity. So it was in ancient Israel, and in the time of the *Tannaim* and the *Amoraim* and the *Geonim*, and partially so in the Golden Age experienced by the Jewish people in Spain. Judaism was never a source of suffering for Israel. Judaism was, for Israel, life in its fullness. No one dreamed of a possible separation between religion and life, as though they were separate or opposing forces.

But the Jewish people underwent a mighty change during the time of the terrible Crusades. The terrible persecutions, the banishment from the different areas of life, the deprivation of breathing space and limitation of movement, seriously damaged the religious strength of the Jew and weakened it. Together with the impoverishment of our life, the scope of our religion became increasingly narrower. Broad, important areas of life were cruelly wrested from our people and its religion. The Hebrew soul was torn to shreds. That joy which results from the total correspondence of spirit and life ceased in Israel. Religion no longer had anything to do with life, and consequently life ceased to be a matter of religion. Concrete living lost its religious form and became a secular matter.

The concept of secular life, which is foreign to the spirit of Israel, came into being during those dark times. The religious sense no longer drew sustenance directly from life …and was sustained only by the fear of death and terror of the severe penalties of the World-to-Come. It is true, of course, that belief in divine reward and punishment is a basic Jewish principle …but extensive use of it, placing it at the center of religious feeling, turning it into the solitary propelling force for fulfilling mitzvot, can plunge a man into depression and induce spiritual malaise.…

This separation from life resulted in the adoption of a negative stance toward life's achievements. The spirit of Israel wore black, donning a cloak of asceticism foreign to the spirit of Judaism. The ghetto stood for hundreds of years, and brought forth great, pious, holy men …who benefited from the splendor of the Torah, and whose thoughts, speech, and deeds were inspired by its holy Presence. But within the ghetto walls lived multitudes who could not taste Torah or be inspired by it. They thirsted for life, and their spirit was crushed by their inability to reach it.…

But one day a new wind began to blow in the world. The ghetto walls fell. Swirling currents of hope for light and freedom, for the prospect of life and productive activity, acquisition of wealth and social standing, flooded the furthest corners of the ghetto and its disenfranchised residents. The thirst for a healthy life, so natural to the Jews …awoke once more with storm and fury. These revolutionary developments brought a crisis upon the congregation of Israel. The one-sided, life-negating religiosity collapsed.… On the one hand stood the elders …who defended with all their might the accepted form of religion, which was based on the negation of life and its achievements, and on the other hand raged the newly liberated from the ghetto-prison, intoxicated and giddy with freedom, who destroyed without scruple all that was precious and sacred in traditional life.

At this time of peril appeared Rav Shimshon Raphael Hirsch of blessed memory and stood in the breach. He stood and proclaimed the ancient truth of Judaism: Religion and life are one and the same.

We can easily see the diametrically opposing positions issuing from the two sources cited here: on the relative importance of *Olam Ha-Zeh* (This World) and *Olam Ha-Ba* (the World-to-Come), on the attitude of Torah Judaism toward productive activity in the social and economic spheres, on life in this world as a treacherous obstacle course or as an exhilarating challenge. Rav Weinberg's conception would undoubtedly strike a sympathetic chord with the people we referred to previously, who find it hard to identify with the view of *Mesilat Yesharim* on these questions. But then what? Faced with this profound difference in world-view, shouldn't we be searching for a way to decide which opinion is correct?

I don't believe that it is to the point to try to arrive at a *pesak* (authoritative halakhic decision) on this matter. The controversy is a given, and the question now is: What is the controversy's significance for us? The important lesson I would learn from this is the very possibility of major differences in outlook within our traditional sources. This lesson itself has an important corollary for the student of Musar. Little progress can be expected from working with a source that provokes strong inner resistance. If there is another approach with which I can identify more easily, why should I, so to speak, knock my head against the wall? Is it necessary to conform to a conceptual framework that does not speak to me? Those who can't accept the approach of *Mesilat Yesharim* still have the option of improving the quality and intensity of their spiritual life by following the approach of Rav Hirsch.

This methodological point about individual choice in Musar study needs to be amplified. Indeed, besides examining the topic at hand, it is important for us to draw out the implications of our analysis for

Musar study in general. We will concentrate more on these broader consequences in our next *shiur*, God willing. But there is one important general comment I should make here, related to the above sources, before resuming our main discussion.

Aside from the fact that the *Mesilat Yesharim* and Rav Weinberg differ in their world-view, there is a basic difference between the *aims* of the two sources. *Mesilat Yesharim* is a classic Musar text; its goal is explicitly didactic. The passage written by Rav Weinberg is descriptive. We may find the prose style stirring or inspiring, but the passage itself asks of the reader no more than intellectual comprehension. How can such a detached, objective piece be of any significance to Musar, which strives for actualization and application?

I would answer by referring to the definition of Musar that I used in the first lesson: study whose *avowed aim* is to learn how to live. According to this definition, the aim of the author of the book is irrelevant; it is the goal of the reader that makes the difference.

One of our greatest luminaries, the Ramban, put this idea tersely in a famous letter to his son that has come to be known as *Iggeret Ha-Musar*, the Epistle of Musar. 'Whenever you get up from a book,' he advised, 'search in what you have learned for something you can fulfill.' That says it all. There are many Torah texts that are not overtly didactic but can yield precious insights when the reading is guided and followed up with the appropriate questions. Rather than seeking objective understanding (what is the author saying? what is the main point?), Ramban would have us ask: What did I get from this? How can this have an impact on my life?

A student of Musar will search for those instances when he can feel the text resonating within himself, pointing a direction toward growth that may become manifest in one's concrete behavior or in one's fundamental orientation. One who assimilates the viewpoint of *Mesilat Yesharim*, for example, relates to life by recognizing trials and pitfalls as part of a pattern that awaits its redeeming explication in the future world. On the other hand, one who responds positively to the conception of Rav Hirsch orients himself to the present life as an end in itself, which awaits its redemption in the here-and-now through the path of Torah.

With this in mind, we will not limit our studies to Musar texts per se, but rather will utilize a wider spectrum of illustrative sources. This is true also of our next excerpt, which was written by Rav Soloveitchik (*Ish Ha-Halakha*, part I, chap. 8).[3] The Rav, of blessed memory, wrote, as a rule, of his own experience and understanding, and avoided an openly didactic posture in matters not strictly halakhic. It seems that mining his wisdom, in particular, requires a personal, searching stance. Here he contrasts the spiritual world of 'halakhic man' to that of the general 'religious man.'

> The difference between halakhic man and religious man is essentially one of orientation; they move in opposite directions. Religious man starts from this world and concludes in *Atzilut* [i.e., the highest metaphysical realm]; Halakhic man begins in *Atzilut* and concludes in this world. Religious man, dissatisfied, disappointed, and unhappy, aspires to ascend from the 'vale of tears' of actuality, to escape the straits of sensed existence, into the divine expanses of transcendental existence, purged and distilled. Halakhic man, to the contrary, yearns to bring transcendence into the 'valley of death' of our world and transform it into the land of life. While religious man throbs with the pining for flight from reality …halakhic man draws a line in the sand of this world and does not leave it. He wishes to purify this world, not to flee it. 'Flight heralds defeat' (*Sota* 8:6). Halakhic man is possessed of a stiffness of neck, a tremendous stubbornness. He battles the evil and the demonic forces of life, and struggles valiantly against the rule of malice and the hosts of wickedness in the world. His mission is directed not toward running away to another world which is all-perfect, but rather to bring down that eternal world into the midst of ours.

Where would you place this world-view, alongside Rabbis Hirsch and Weinberg, or together with *Mesilat Yesharim*? Clearly, halakhic man does not see *Olam Ha-Ba* as his desired destination. To the contrary, he scorns the impulse to 'flee' from this world. This would connect him to the ideal outlined by Rav Weinberg. Yet halakhic man's point of departure seems strikingly similar to that of *Mesilat Yesharim*. He is not enthralled by 'the prospect of light and freedom' extended by this world. He holds this world to be a vale of tears, a valley of death, inhabited by demonic forces and malicious hosts. But his conclusion is still thoroughly different from that of *Mesilat Yesharim*.

We have seen, then, that the relationship of *Olam Ha-Zeh* and *Olam Ha-Ba* admits various attitudes. This is one of the questions determining the direction of our spiritual life and activity. Our claim here is that discovering the approach that is right for a given individual can be crucial if he is to progress religiously. In our next lesson, we will further develop the theme of individual adaptation as we continue to examine the relationship of the physical and spiritual realms of existence.

## Notes

1.  As mentioned in our first shiur, we will be quoting illustrative sources extensively. In the interest of fairness, I should note a drawback inherent in this technique. Our quotations necessarily will be partial, and therefore will not always accurately reflect the complete viewpoint of their authors. The passage here cited, for example, does not do justice to the *Mesilat Yesharim*, which is not a monolithic work. Since our aim here is to help people grapple with Musar, I presume that Ramchal, the author of *Mesilat Yesharim*, would agree to bear with us.
2.  Rav Yechiel Yaakov Weinberg, Seridei Eish, vol. 4, pp. 365–366.
3.  What follows is my translation from the Hebrew. The English reader may refer to Lawrence Kaplan's rendition, Halakhic Man (Jewish Publication Society).

# Shiur three

# *Olam Ha-Zeh, Olam Ha-Ba –* This World and the Next

## PART II

IN OUR LAST *shiur,* we began developing two themes simultaneously. Our direct concern was to examine the orientation of our sources – and ourselves – to the world we inhabit: Is it a place in which to be at home, or should it arouse the desire to be elsewhere? Together with this first issue, we considered the ramifications of what we have seen so far for the study of Musar in general. Before learning more about the relationship between this world and the World-to-Come, I would like to begin by picking up the thread of one of our general conclusions about Musar.

As you will recall, we raised the question of individual choice of texts and approaches. Our encounter with various sources that posited vastly differing views on important matters drew us to a vital inference: Since we cannot adopt more than one of the views, we would be well advised to develop our spiritual lives in accordance with the approach with which we identify closely.

It is interesting to note that the dilemma of fitting the text to the reader was delineated by the Alte Rebbe, Rav Shneur Zalman of Lyady, in the introduction to his classic Chasidic text, the *Tanya*:

It is well known and commonly acknowledged by all our colleagues that there is no comparison between hearing words of Musar and the reading of books, which are read by the reader according to his own way and understanding.... If his mind and mood are confused, walking in darkness regarding the service of God, he will hardly see the good light that is concealed in those books, sweet and soul- healing though it be. Also, books about piety that are based on human intelligence are definitely not appropriate for everyone, because not everyone is of the same mind, and what causes one person's mind to stir and become aroused will not affect another's mind in the same way.... Even books about piety that are based on the holy sources, the midrashim of Chazal, in whom the spirit of God spoke and His word was upon their tongue, and even considering that the Torah and the Holy One are as One, and all the six hundred thousand souls of the Congregation of Israel (down to the last individual, even until the slightest spark of the of the simplest of our people, Benei Yisrael) are all bound to the Torah, and the Torah binds them to the Holy One, as is known from the Zohar – but all this is true only in general terms. And even though the Torah was designed to be understood in general, but also individually, by every single soul of Israel rooted in it, not everyone is able to know his individual place in Torah.

The *Tanya* distinguishes between a student who engages his human teacher in direct discourse and a student whose 'teacher' is a book. The book was written without knowing the person who reads it. Its content is suited to its author, but its potential effect on the random reader cannot be predicted. This is certainly true of works based on human insight and understanding, however inspired. But, continues the Alte Rebbe, the problem of individual appropriateness exists even when the content is based on insights gathered from Torah texts. This latter claim is interesting. The *Tanya* bases his statement on a mystical doctrine concerning the individual root of each Jewish soul in the Torah, which implies that no person's grasp of Torah is exactly like another person's. But does this mean that I can't just take any Torah text and learn it, without checking first to see that it is 'for me'?

If we pay careful attention to what Rav Shneur Zalman says, we see that he is concerned primarily with 'books of piety,' that is, Musar. It is precisely here that individual proclivity is so important a factor that it poses a serious question to the reader: Is this book, idea, or directive – 'mine'? Do I identify with it sufficiently to benefit from it, to grow with it? As we saw in our first *shiurim*, one of the distinguishing traits of Musar is its individuality.[1]

To sum up, the *Tanya* recognizes the gap between text and student as a psychological reality grounded in metaphysics. The potential for such a gap is an inherent characteristic of Musar texts. As such, encountering it should be expected as a matter of course. No serious study of Musar can ignore this phenomenon.

From here we return to our initial observation. If our experience with a given text is one of dissonance, searching elsewhere is a reasonable strategy. However, a word of caution is in order. There clearly is a danger here of 'censorship.' It is not always wise to set aside an entire text because one does not identify with certain aspects of it. Using the example of *Mesilat Yesharim*: even those who find themselves at variance with the work's above-mentioned views regarding *Olam Ha-Zeh* may still have much to gain from the book as a whole. Also, excessive use of the individualistic approach could conceivably degenerate into a cavalier attitude that dismisses difficult challenges with a shrugging 'This doesn't suit me.' Nevertheless, I think that, in general, anyone who is concerned with enhancing his spiritual life is not averse to taking up challenges, and should not suspect himself wrongly of trying to go easy on himself. Bearing the qualifications in mind, the over- arching consideration remains that I must identify with a message before I can motivate myself to adopt and apply it.

Let us get back to the topic of *Olam Ha-Zeh*, the physical world, about which we have already glimpsed three opinions. Our next source is a relevant short remark of the Vilna Gaon, which comes down to us in a well-known homily delivered by his disciple, Rav

Chayim of Volozhin, during the High Holiday season, on the subject of repentance:[2]

> It is therefore worthwhile, during these Days of Awe, for every Jew to pray mainly for his miserable soul, that it not perish, Heaven forbid. Unfortunately, in our many sins, the evil inclination blinds the eyes of the masses of people, and puts a retort in their mouths in the form of a platitude that everyone repeats: 'This world is also a world, and it too needs attention.' In fact, such a statement may be appropriately made by men of great piety, who serve God with love, and with no extraneous intention. I have heard so several times from the holy mouth of our master, the saintly Gaon Eliyahu of blessed memory: 'What importance does the World-to-Come have? One cannot serve God with love there, nor do anything to please our Creator and Maker. This world is the main one. That is why the Rabbis said, 'One moment of repentance and good deeds in this world is worth more than all the life of the World-to-Come.' (This I heard from the Gaon,) but as for us, lowly of worth, how could we presume to abandon the spiritual life in favor of the corporeal?

The Gaon expressed his deeply felt conviction that this world, with its 'corporeal life,' is inestimably worthwhile in comparison to the next. This feeling surely emanated from the intense fulfillment he experienced when doing God's will. His student, Rav Chayim, denied that ordinary people could make such a statement authentically. When the man in the street talks about this world, he doesn't mean Torah and mitzvot, but much more mundane activities. Hence, when addressing the masses, Rav Chayim of Volozhin asserts that *Olam Ha-Ba* must be projected as the ideal.

Of course, as far as the basic issue goes, it is clear that Rav Chayim himself identifies with the view of his teacher. On this main point, it would be instructive to compare the Gaon to Rav Hirsch and to Rav Soloveitchik. They all assess *Olam Ha-Zeh* as the quintessential place of human fulfillment, but do they all do so in the same way? Also, what would Rav Hirsch and Rav Soloveitchik say about Rav Chayim's distinction between the great man and the ordinary man? I leave these questions for the reader's consideration.

We will examine one more formulation of a stance taken on this issue. The following excerpt is from *Mei Marom* (vol. 7, chap. 6), by Rav Yaakov Moshe Charlop, one of the foremost students of Rav Kook:

> At first glance, it would seem that the thought of the future is the main factor in life. The more we envision a hopeful future, the more conscientious we are about fulfilling everything…. All of life is viewed as an existence that can bring about a wonderful future, as a means to an end. But although our Sages of blessed memory …said, 'One moment of satisfaction in the World-to-Come is worth more than all the life of this world,' they were still wise enough to tell us that 'One moment of repentance and good deeds in this world is worth more than all the life of the World-to-Come.' This is no mere figure of speech, but the word of God speaking truly in their mouths. As great and awesome as are the beneficial *effects* of Torah and mitzvot (namely, attaining the glory and delight of the World-to-Come), greater and even more exalted are the very *acts* of the mitzvot, the learning of the Torah *itself*, the repentance *itself*, and the good deeds *themselves*. This difference in greatness is comparable to the difference between the effect of the Good and the Good itself. Although from a utilitarian viewpoint, one may benefit more from the effect of the Good, yet as far as absolute value is concerned, the unknowable Good itself is certainly of greater value than the effect that emanates *from* the Good. So it is with the value of the benefits that stem from Torah and mitzvot as compared to their fulfillment (which is inconceivable outside of this world): there is no comparison between the value of the thing itself and the value of whatever branches out from it.…
>
> It follows that the consciousness of the present, of the greatness of the elevated thought that recognizes the Good itself prior to its spreading forth, and understands that one moment of repentance and good deeds in this world is worth more than all the life of the World-to-Come, is much higher and more exalted than the con-

sciousness of the future, even the purest and most exalted future. Our duty is to purify ourselves and work hard to reach that level where all life is not only *causative* life but *essential* life; not only life as a means but life as an end, Divine life.

Here again it is instructive to compare Rav Charlop's position with the others we have seen. And again I will leave this to you. I would like to concentrate for a moment, not so much on content, but on the distinctive style of the foregoing passage. It clearly bears the mark of Rav Charlop's background in philosophy and Kabbalah. It calls upon the reader to respond inwardly to, and identify with, an abstract concept, the Good, which we can perhaps define as absolute morality of Divine origin. The reader's positive response to this passage will be commensurate to the extent that he 'knows' what Rav Charlop is talking about, although this knowledge cannot be more than intuitive. If Rav Charlop has struck an empathetic chord with you, you may sense the exaltation that clearly moves him.

This brings us to another general observation. Different sources that deal with a given topic can differ not only in *what* they say, but *how* they say it. Sometimes the effect a text has upon the reader is not only a matter of rational identification with the message, but depends on the reader's receptiveness to the author's mode of expression. Two authors may say the same thing, but only one will 'strike home.' This, in turn, can depend on various factors, such as personality and background. But there is one set of influencing factors that I would like especially to mention.

One's ability to be affected by a given text can depend on factors that are *temporary*. For example, what mood am I in: contemplative? agitated? depressed? placid? spiritual or 'mystical'? Whatever my state, I may feel the need for a text that speaks to my present condition. Or to the contrary, I may find that something which is the opposite of my present mood will be most effective, something that will balance my condition or take me out of it.

Likewise, a given source may or may not evoke a meaningful response on my part because of the stage of life I am at. People change.

The same person may find himself impervious, say, to classic Musar works or to *Chassidut* while in his late teens, and discover a few years later that he has developed a receptivity, or even a need, for them. The same can be true of any text or class of texts. We are all familiar with the phenomenon of schools of thought and lifestyle in traditional Judaism. There are Breslovers, Litvaks, Lubavitchers, Merkaznikim, and more, and even among those mentioned there are subdivisions. These groups represent communities of people who ostensibly have 'found' their way, who will live out their lives according to a given mold and do not expect to change. They will be nurtured spiritually by the literature and lore connected with their group, and will not be significantly affected by currents from the outside. Or at least so it would seem. Is this an accurate description of the state of affairs? If so, is it genuine, or does it have a large degree of artificiality, owing to the human need for stability and a sense of belonging? I confess that I often wonder about this.

My own impression is that alongside the tendency for people to label themselves, there is a growing trend toward cross-pollination of ideas even among the insulated. People change, and as they change, they are wont to reach out for wisdom that is not readily found within the confines of their familiar environment. I agree that insularity was more real and more possible years ago. Today, with the tremendous exposure to the wealth of ideas generated by our tradition, it appears to me to be less plausible.

Of course, there are undoubtedly many whose religious life finds true and total expression in one lifestyle, such as those I mentioned. If you are a person of this type, there is certainly nothing wrong with that. You could be considered fortunate, and I am sure that many would envy you. But speaking to the others, who I believe are the majority, be aware that you can benefit from many different viewpoints and modes of thought and expression. Be mindful that your spiritual inclinations and needs can change. A working knowledge of what different texts have to offer may turn out to be an important resource.

Here we will close our discussion of *Olam Ha-Zeh* and *Olam Ha-Ba*. I hope that you have gained an appreciation of some of the divergent treatments of this issue, and that our survey has helped you examine your own thoughts on the matter. Our *shiurim* thus far have tried to help define what Musar is: a very personal, individual study- search that constantly confronts us with the necessity to choose what is right for us, and to commit ourselves to our choices. We will, *be-ezrat Hashem*, continue to address this process – its technique, and the obstacles along the way.

In our next lesson, we will begin to tackle one of the central issues of Musar literature: *ga'ava* and *anava* – pride and humility.

## Notes

1. See further in the *Tanya*, where he points out that this principle is relevant to Halakhic study as well, albeit to a lesser extent.
2. Drashat Maharach, Jerusalem 5731, pp. 12–13. As the following citation demonstrates, Rav Chaim often felt the need to discern between ideas which were suited for mass consumption and those whose popularization could be self-defeating. Rav Chaim's son, Rav Yitzchak of Volozhin, dwelt on this in his introduction to his father's work Nefesh Ha-Chaim.

# Shiur four

# *Anava* (Humility)

## PART I

O<small>UR TRADITION</small> places great emphasis on humility as an ethical ideal. This often confronts the serious student with a dilemma whose resolution is of critical importance. The dilemma issues from the apparently paradoxical role played by *anava* (humility) in the general field of spiritual activity. On the one hand, *anava* occupies a special place among the various character traits extolled in Musar literature. Anyone familiar with our sources knows that *anava* is regarded as one of the most important, if not *the* most important, of desirable *midot* (character traits), and that its opposite, *ga'ava* (pride), is seen as particularly pernicious, even revolting. The Rambam, for example, recommends in *Hilkhot De'ot* that we follow the 'middle way' with respect to personal characteristics. And yet he writes (chap. 2, para. 3):

> However, there are some traits with regard to which one may not conduct oneself intermediately, but rather should distance oneself from one extreme and adopt the opposite extreme. Specifically, this is true regarding haughtiness; for it is not good for a person to be merely meek, but rather he should be humble of spirit, and his spirit should be exceedingly low. For this reason Scripture calls Moshe Rabbenu 'very humble,' not merely 'humble.' Therefore the Sages commanded: 'Be very, very lowly of spirit.' They also said

that he who raises his heart is denying God, as it is written, 'Lest your heart become high, and you forget the Lord your God.' And they also said: 'The ban should be placed on anyone who has even a little arrogance.'

What is the reason for this special emphasis? For our purposes, I would single out the relevance of this particular *mida* to our general area of study. The whole idea of working to achieve *tikkun* (self-correction) is based on the premise that at present all is not right with oneself. To the extent that a person remains unmindful of his shortcomings, he does not believe that he really needs to correct anything. Arrogance, then, is the nemesis of Musar. The thought that 'I am basically fine, but anyone can stand a little improvement' will not generate the willpower to make major changes. A powerful drive for spiritual progress can grow only from the soil of humility.

Paradoxically, however, humility itself may often be counted among the impediments to religious growth. Frequently, *anava* is used to justify a state of torpor, an attitude of laziness and despair inimical to any sort of meaningful activity, including Musar. One who has succumbed to this phenomenon is certain that his attitude is the praiseworthy outcome of his humility. I would like to illustrate how this can happen with a passage by a modern-day author, Rav Yisrael Hess ל"ז, who wrote a popularly oriented Musar book called *Derekh Ha-Avoda*. Prior to the following citation (pp. 66–67), the author had been leading the reader in a search for the 'I':

> Who, then, am I? Not my body, my mind, my other spiritual capacities, not even my will. We have searched for the *ani* ('I'), but we have not found it. Perhaps, then, there is no I.
>
> Wonderful – congratulations! At long last we discover that there is no *ani*, but there is *ayin* (nothing). This actual nothing, while descending from the world of absolute truth into this world of falsehood and confusion, became so distorted and confused that the order of the letters of the word which designates our essence, *ayin*, became distorted and disordered into the lie that there is an *ani*....
>
> This requires explanation. We know from the Prophets that the

glory of God fills the world…. If the existence of God is present in all the worlds and fills them, then there is no place vacant of Him, and it follows that there can be no existence other than Him in the world. Any reality that takes up a place in the world, of necessity, pushes away the Holy One, who until now occupied that place. Of course, we are not talking about, God forbid, a physical reality, as though Divinity were to occupy physical space in the world and the space that occupies, say, a stone, pushes God away. We are, of course, talking about a *feeling*. Any created thing should feel itself as totally null vis-à-vis its Creator. Anything that feels itself to be an independent entity, existing separately from God and standing autonomously, is demonstrating (by this very feeling of existence which does not nullify itself before God) that there is, so to speak, another entity in the world besides God, and this is what is tantamount to pushing away the Divine Presence. On the other hand, any created thing that while physically existing and occupying physical space in the world, still does not feel itself as an entity, nullifies its existence before God, and is not autonomous and independent – that creature is void and does not take up the place of its Creator.

Further on (p. 75), the author applies this approach to the definition of evil:

It follows that the evil in the world results only from the lack of self-nullification before God, and is to be found only in one who feels and acts as an independent entity that exists unto itself. Whoever utilizes his free choice and actualizes the option given him at the moment of his creation to sense himself as a separate entity, he is the doer of evil. Hence, when we say that God created evil, we are saying that God created man with the option of seeing himself as a separate entity…. This feeling of existence is what we have called 'I,' the sense that there is an I which is not null. Hence, 'God created evil' equals 'God created me with the feeling of I'; in other words, 'I' = evil.

This presentation appears to be following the theory of *anava* to its inexorable conclusion. God is everything, and therefore I am truly nothing. One who assimilates this viewpoint is, ostensibly, virtually inoculated against arrogance. But many well-meaning people react to this argument with protest.

I don't know what Rav Hess's approach 'does' to you, but I know that many feel that it attacks their religiosity. In candor, I understand them very well. Jews have many commandments to perform. In fact, the essence of being Jewish – perhaps the essence of being human, in the Jewish view – is being commanded. The tasks that God expects us to perform are at times exceedingly difficult. Can a 'nothing' be commanded? Can a nullity be expected to exercise self-control in trying situations, or to toil mightily in Torah study or altruistic endeavors? Doesn't success in Torah imply, and require, not nothingness, but greatness?[1]

Extolling the virtues of self-nullification seems to entail the danger of passivity, and tends to excuse man's low spiritual achievement as a necessary result of his lack of inherent value. But then what? If we can't live with the idea of self-nullification, do we dismiss humility as a desired goal? Clearly, abandoning the idea of *anava* altogether is not an option. This issue is so central that anyone interested in Musar must formulate for himself a clear and workable approach to it.

We will not examine here the questions of whether Rav Hess's argument can be found in the sources, and of the extent to which the sources justify his conclusion in the realm of practical ethics. I would rather try to develop an alternative definition of humility, different from the foregoing, and not based on its philosophic premise. On this occasion I will stray from my usual eclectic attitude and take a clear stand.

I believe that the author of the Musar classic, *Chovot Ha-Levavot* (Sha'ar Ha-Kenia 9), alludes to a different conception of humility in the following passage, in which he deals with pride based on spiritual achievement:

> Pride over spiritual attainments can be of two types, one disgraceful and the other praiseworthy. It is disgraceful if a person is proud of

his wisdom or the righteous man of his deeds, if this makes whatever he already has of them to be much in his eyes, and makes him think that the good name and high opinion which he has among men is enough for him, and makes him belittle and despise others and speak ill of them, and causes the wise and great of his generation to be unworthy in his eyes, and causes him to gloat over the faults and folly of his comrades. This is what our Sages of blessed memory called 'honoring oneself through the disgrace of one's fellow-man.' A person such as we have described is neither meek nor humble.

But the praiseworthy type is when a person is proud of his wisdom or the righteous man of his deeds, and considers them a great favor of the Creator for which to be thankful and joyous, and this causes him to try to add on to them, to be humble with his near ones and enjoy his friends, and to be considerate of their honor, to conceal their folly and speak their praise …and all his good deeds are few in his eyes, and he constantly works to increase them, and is humble because of his inability to do as much as he would like…. This pride does no harm to humility and does not keep it distant. Of this pride Scripture says in connection with Yehoshafat, 'His heart was high in the ways of God.' This pride assists humility, and adds to it, as it is written, 'humility brings about fear of God.'

The discussion in *Chovot Ha-Levavot* is based on a very instructive premise: that not all pride is bad. We are not yet able to understand all of what he tells us, but he clearly thinks that there are two ways of being proud: one of them is antithetical to humility, and the other not only does not conflict with humility, but actually assists and strengthens it. Rav Kook, in a collection of brief ethical observations called *Midot Ha-Re'iya*,[2] made the same point (*Ga'ava* 25):

He who would penetrate the profound hidden reaches of his soul must carefully assess the feeling of pride, that illegitimate feeling which can cause him to behave against his own better judgment as well as that of his Maker, and which is the refined feeling that enlarges the human spirit and reminds man of his full, glorious, spiritual essence.

If only we knew how to make the distinction!

I think we can be helped here by once again enlisting the aid of Rav Kook (ibid., *Kavod* 4):

> To the extent of the lack of inner perfection, nature will strive for exterior perfection. Only from a state of baseness of spirit will awaken the drive for self-glorification before others, whether in what the spirit really has or in what it does not have. Therefore, man must increase the impression of inner perfection, and then his words, when speaking of himself before others, will always be properly balanced.

Rav Kook defines the motive for self-glorification. It is not, as one might think, the result of a positive self-appraisal which, not content with its own opinion, demands the agreement and recognition of others. The deeper root of the need for honor is a paucity of spirit, which Rav Kook tellingly describes as the lack of 'the *impression* of inner perfection.' If I understand him correctly, Rav Kook is saying that *lack of self-esteem* is the psychological basis of arrogance. For only one who is unconvinced of his inherent worth will feel the need to find artificial compensation in approval from without – what Rav Kook terms 'exterior perfection.'

This is not to say that false pride will necessarily result in addiction to praise from others. There are subtler expressions. A good friend once told me, 'Do you know what *ga'ava* is? It's when you're in a room full of acquaintances, and you go through them in your mind, saying to yourself: I'm smarter than this one, I'm a better friend than that one, I'm more industrious than the next, and so on.' It doesn't matter whether the caress comes from others or from myself, the addictive preoccupation is the same. This is the giveaway of *ga'ava*. *Ga'ava* is the compulsive quest for honor.

The antithesis of *ga'ava* is not the 'humility' that says, 'I am truly nothing.' On the contrary, it is true, liberating self-esteem; this is the 'praiseworthy pride' of the *Chovot Ha-Levavot*. A Jew, in particular, knows that the Master of the Universe has great expectations of him. How could such weighty, spiritual demands be made of anyone other than a being with a Divine soul, with a profound potential for a life-time of moral feeling and activity, a being of the utmost significance? If I truly believe what I profess to believe, I don't need anyone's approval. Compliments and recognition are irrelevant. The inner richness of one's personality is more than sufficient; the only concern is, Am I doing enough? Am I fulfilling my destiny?

This last sentence brings us to the question which I am sure you wanted to ask. If the antithesis of *ga'ava* is self-esteem, what is humility? Why are we supposed to be 'very, very lowly of spirit'? The answer is that if we are convinced of the greatness of our Divine-human soul to the point of no concern about its verification, we will necessarily be confronted with the stark reality that our lives until now have not remotely approached the level which such a soul could attain.

Remember what the *Chovot Ha-Levavot* said? Negative pride results in one's thinking that the wisdom and good deeds one has already attained 'are much in his eyes.' Where does this thought come from? From lack of self-esteem; from the conviction that I am really incapable of doing much that is worthwhile, and if I have managed to get anywhere, I truly deserve approbation, because it was above and beyond what could be reasonably expected from someone like me. At any rate, the idea of further achievement would be absurd and out of character.

On the other hand, positive pride actually *assists* humility. This is because positive pride comes from self- esteem. No matter how much I have done that is worthwhile, it will never be enough, because I know myself well enough to realize that I could have done much more. Thus is genuine humility inspired – the thought that 'all his good deeds are few in his eyes.' Positive attainments are considered not, mainly, as confirmation of one's worth (for this is scarcely necessary), but as confirmation of what can and remains to be done.

To sum up: humility (*anava*) = self-esteem; arrogance (*ga'ava*) = lack of self-esteem. Recall that we opened this *shiurim* by posing the dilemma of how to arrive at a definition of humility that would en-courage *tikkun* rather than stunt it. We conclude, after having offered our definition of *anava*, with a different dilemma: the psychological fault- line of intrinsic self-worth, on the one hand, versus the sense of inadequate fulfillment, on the other. The two poles are logically interdependent, though they are bound to conflict experientially even as they fortify each other. This is a healthy conflict. It is, perhaps, the fundamental conflict of religious man.

I think enough has been said about this for one sitting. In our next *shiur*, God willing, we will follow up the definition of *anava* with a discussion of some of its further implications.

## Notes

1.  At this point I call attention once more to the problematic aspect of partial quotations. I raised this matter in the footnote to lesson 2. In this case, however, I believe that Rav Hess's position is rather well represented by the passages quoted here.
2.  *Midot Ha-Reiya* was published together with Rav Kook's *Musar Avikha*.

# Shiur five

# *Anava* (Humility)

## PART II

WE WILL BEGIN by recapping the gist of our last *shiur*. We argued that there are two attitudes that may be called pride but in reality are totally different from one another: self-esteem and arrogance. When the sources denigrate *ga'ava*, we claimed, they are referring only to the second; the first, upon examination, turns out to be the basis of humility. Conversely, praiseworthy humility is always associated with healthy self-esteem. Lack of self-esteem leads to the damaging feeling of worthlessness.

I would like to cite a few more statements made by Rav Kook in *Midot Ha-Re'iya* that illustrate this. The first example contrasts the psychological effects of the two types of *anava* (*Anava* 11):

> Genuine humility and lowliness increase health and vitality, whereas the imaginary [humility] causes illness and melancholy. Therefore, one ought to choose for oneself the traits of humility and lowliness in their clear form, and thus become strong and valiant.

Here we are given a rule of thumb for distinguishing true humility from its bogus look-alike (ibid. 7):

> Whenever humility brings about melancholy, it is invalid. But when it is worthy, it engenders joy, courage, and inner glory.

Rav Kook has this to say about the relation of self- esteem and humility (ibid. 8):

> At times we should not be afraid of the feeling of greatness, which elevates man to do great things. And all humility is based on such a holy feeling of greatness.

Let us now take the discussion further. The groundwork we have laid requires us to elaborate on two problems our approach seems to arouse. The first is an apparent paradox implicit in our definitions of *anava* and *ga'ava*. We diagnosed *ga'ava* (arrogance) as stemming from lack of self-esteem – the wallowing preoccupation with one's past achievements that is needed to compensate for the missing conviction of self-worth. Yet, on the other hand, lack of self-esteem can also lead to the opposite pole: a person lacking self-esteem is wont to conclude that he really is without worth as a person. Shouldn't that, at least, be considered humility? Can such an individual be faulted with *ga'ava*?

The answer is that when self-esteem is gone, the addiction to praise is virtually unavoidable. It is certainly there, even in the supposedly humble man. The fact that a person is convinced of his nothingness does not commend him as an *anav,* to whom honor is meaningless; it merely means that he has despaired of getting the adulation he sorely wants, from others or from himself, on the basis of positive accomplishment. Therefore, he seeks refuge in the one illusion of achievement that is within his grasp: being an *anav.* The distorted mind thinks that humility, one of the highest virtues, can be had easily. In this view, one need not even attempt to actually do anything worthwhile, for the mark of the humble person is that he does not have the arrogance to believe himself capable of anything. Cowardice masquerading as virtue, obsession with honor configured to resemble lowliness of spirit, the hollow illusion of effortless achievement paraded as a substitute for true self-worth – these are the characteristics of one who facilely declares himself to be nothing. Genuine *anava*, on the other hand, says, 'I am capable of doing much more, and therefore I must.'

Illustrations from the lives of the *gedolei Yisrael* abound. Think of the Chafetz Chayim, a man of legendary humility. Does it seem anomalous to you that a humble person would consider himself worthy of writing the encyclopedic *Mishna Berura*, in which he takes it upon himself to decide for *Klal Yisrael* in all halakhic matters pertaining to daily life, and to be the arbiter between all previous authorities, such as the *Magen Avraham* and the *Pri Megadim*? In fact, we possess the personal record of Rabbenu Bachaye ibn Pakuda, author of the ground-breaking *Chovot Ha-Levavot*, who writes (in the introduction) that he found himself facing this anomaly:

> When I planned to execute my decision to write this book, I saw that one like me is unworthy of writing a book such as this. I surmised that my ability would not suffice to analyze all the necessary aspects, owing to the difficulty which I perceived and to my wisdom being insufficient and my mind being too weak to grasp all of the issues, and that I am not fluent in the Arabic language in which I wrote it (that being the language best understood by most people today). I feared that I would toil at something that would evidence my inability, and that it would be a presumptuous undertaking, so that I considered changing my mind and abandoning my previous decision.

Rabbenu Bachaye tells us quite frankly that his 'humility' at this point was really concerned with 'how will it look' ('something that would evidence my inability'). Fortunately for all succeeding generations, he was perceptive enough to overcome his 'modesty:'

> But when I designed to remove this laborious burden from myself and desist from composing the work, I reconsidered and became suspicious of myself for having chosen to rest and to dwell in the abode of laziness in peace and tranquility, and I feared that it was the desire of the [evil] passion which was placing this thought [within me], and that it was he who was diverting me to the way of composure and peace ...and I knew that many minds have been lost out of apprehension, and many losses have been caused by fear. And I remembered what someone said: 'Vigilance dictates that one not be excessively vigilant.' ...And I said, if all those involved in good

causes and teachers of the straight and correct path were to remain silent and still until they could completely attain their ideal, no man would ever say a word after the Prophets of blessed memory, who were chosen by God and strengthened by His help.... And I realized that people have a great natural desire for ill purposes, and are negligent in the ways of kindness, and behave with laziness when it comes to advancing good.... And when they see an object of desire, they invent falsehoods in order to justify their inclination to it, and they rely on those arguments to sustain and strengthen their [natural] inclination.

Rabbenu Bachaye's account of false modesty unmasked, speaks for itself.

The second issue that needs to be clarified has to do with another of the central concepts of Jewish ethics: guilt. When I use this term, I am of course referring not to the objective fact of guilt (so-and-so is guilty of theft, etc.), but to guilt as a subjective feeling. Unlike the modern view, which sees guilt feelings as unnecessary psychological baggage, our tradition views them as an essential component of *teshuva* (repentance). Rabbenu Yona, an early Musar (and halakhic) authority, claims that the quality of *teshuva* is a function of the depth of guilt (*Sha'arei Teshuva* 1.12):

The level of the penitence and its merits are in relation to the degree of the bitterness and the force of the agony [felt by the penitent]. This is the penitence that comes by way of purity of the spirit and clarity of the mind. For the greater the mind, the more the eyes are opened; the agony of thought should likewise increase exceedingly.... For agony [over sin] comes from the purity of the uppermost soul, and the soul is again accepted [by God], more than it would have been as a result of physical suffering and pain.

If we consider feelings of profound guilt to be ethically desirable, we must ask what thoughts and attitudes bring them about. I suspect that many people would answer that the 'guilty' person is the one who thinks that his life is devoid of worthy accomplishment, ridden with iniquity, and, above all, takes the foregoing as proof of his total worthlessness as a person. The depth of guilt is taken to be in direct relation to the attitude of self-nullification. Doesn't the self-esteem that we have been advocating preclude genuine guilt?

While interpreting guilt as a 'declaration of nothingness' has a superficial and melodramatic appeal, it is just as deceptive as the same interpretation with respect to humility. The truth is that a person without self-esteem is completely incapable of genuine guilt. Can a cripple be faulted for not running a marathon? How can I blame myself for any shortcoming after having convinced myself of my impotence?

Rav Soloveitchik זצ"ל once pointed out that Chazal had an odd term for the declaration which the Halakha requires to be made every three years after one has discharged the duty of tithes: they called it *vidui ma'asrot*, literally meaning 'confession regarding tithes.' The content of the declaration is:

> I have removed the sacred produce from my home, and have given it to the Levite, the stranger, the orphan, and the widow, in exact accordance with Your commandment of me; I have not transgressed Your commandment, and I have not forgotten it…. I have done all that You commanded me. (Devoir 26:13–14)

Hardly what one could call a confession! The Rav suggested that by calling this a *vidui*, the Sages wished to impress upon us that any confession of sin must include, in order to be meaningful, the realization that one is a spiritual being with spiritual achievements. Only then can one really feel the weight of sin. Only then can one honestly say, as is customary on Yom Kippur eve, *temehim anu al nafshotenu* – We are astonished at ourselves, how could we possibly have behaved in a way that so unbecomes us?

I believe that the barrier which self-nullification poses to self-rectification is at the core of a particularly dramatic Biblical episode that I will now try to analyze (Shemuel I, chap. 15). Judgmental treatment of such a great figure as Shaul is not to be engaged in without trepidation. However, the Biblical account was written for us to learn from; let us proceed in that spirit.

Shaul has returned from his successful battle against Amalek. He is met by the prophet Shemuel, who at God's bidding had sent Shaul on the mission. Shaul is exultant: 'Blessed are you unto God. I have upheld God's word!'

In this jubilant atmosphere, Shemuel is faced with the unpleasant task of pointing out the reality: Shaul's failure to do his duty. Shemuel tactfully tries to change the mood: 'And what is that sound of sheep in my ears, and the sound of cattle that I hear?'

Shemuel is trying to conjure up the words that he had used to send Shaul on his way. Shaul had been commanded to 'have no mercy', and kill all the Amalekites and their livestock, 'every ox and sheep, every camel and donkey.' However, Shaul, evidently oblivious to the allusion, answers: 'The men brought them from the Amalekites, for they had mercy on the best of the sheep and the cattle, in order to sacrifice them to the Lord your God; and the rest, we destroyed.'

The dialogue unfolds as follows:

> And Shemuel said to Shaul, 'Be silent and I will tell you what God has said to me this night'; and he said to him, 'Speak.'
>
> And Shemuel said, 'See, though you are small in your eyes, you are the head of the tribes of Israel, and God has anointed you as king over Israel. And God sent you on a path, saying, 'Go and wipe out the sinners, Amalek, and fight them until you have destroyed them.' Why did you not heed God's voice, but went after the spoils and did evil in the eyes of God?'
>
> And Shaul said to Shemuel, 'Truly I heeded the voice of God, and I went on the way which God has sent me. I brought Agag, the king of Amalek, and Amalek I destroyed. And the men took from the spoils sheep and cattle, the best of the take, to sacrifice to the Lord your God at Gilgal.'
>
> And Shemuel said, 'Does God desire burnt offerings and sacrifices as much as He desires the heeding of His voice? Now obedience is better than sacrifice, harkening than the fat of rams. For disobedience is as sinful as witchcraft, and obstinacy is as evil as idolatry. Since you have despised the word of God, He has despised your kingship.'

> And Shaul said to Shemuel, 'I have sinned, for I transgressed the mouth of God and your words, for I feared the men, and I heeded their voice.'

The most puzzling aspect of this dialogue is Shaul's prolonged insistence that he is blameless. Not only does Shemuel's first statement fail to elicit a confession, but even his explicit rebuke merely prompts Shaul to once again claim that he has faithfully discharged his mission. Only after Shemuel tells him that God no longer wants him to reign does Shaul break down and admit the truth. Why?

I think we can understand this if we notice the diagnosis of Shaul's sin as recorded in this conversation. Shaul says of himself, 'I feared the men, and I heeded their voice.' Shemuel says to him, 'Though you are small in your eyes, you are the head of the tribes of Israel.' One is the outgrowth of the other. Shaul feared the men because he was small in his own eyes.

Imagine one who is small in his own eyes, who is unsure of his self-worth, and then is appointed king of Israel. How does he relate to this office? There is a right way, and a wrong way. The right way is to set aside all self-doubt. There can be no greater personal assurance than the fact that God Himself has chosen him for this unique position. With his self-esteem affirmed and strengthened, with his ego unthreatened, the king sets out to perform his appointed task 'for the sake of Heaven.'

But there is a wrong way, the way for which Shaul is now being chastised. He allows the evil inclination toward self-doubt to persist even after he becomes king. Now the kingship means something else altogether; the king who is small in his own eyes must use his kingship to *prove* himself, to protect his insecure ego. The allegiance of the people becomes his addiction. He is not motivated to serve in the capacity of king for the benefit of his people or to do God's will. Rather, he holds on to his crown for dear life, for without it he is worth nothing.

Shaul was faced with the prospect of mutiny among his troops. He was aware that the order to refrain from despoiling would be a test of his leadership. Had Shaul been executing his mandate of kingship properly, he would have had the self-confidence to do everything he could to enforce discipline. He would have been willing to risk failure, because God expects him only to do what he can. But Shaul feared the men because he *needed* to be king. If they flouted his will, he would no longer be the king, and the peg on which he had hung his self-worth would be gone. He could not afford to put himself to the test.

But now Shaul found himself in a bind. For while he could not bring himself to risk the disobedience of his troops, neither could he admit, to himself or to anyone else, that he was afraid to take the risk. For this very fear was itself the cruelest evidence that Shaul was, in fact, not the king. A true king enforces his decisions and does not worry about disgruntled subjects. Facing up to his fear would mean admitting that he was ruled and manipulated by his soldiers. The crown on his head would be exposed as hollow and meaningless. That is why he could not accept responsibility, even when the facts were placed plainly before him.

If our understanding is correct, it also clarifies what ultimately enabled Shaul to confess. It was the discovery that his behavior had caused God to desire the cancellation of his reign. Now he saw the futility of all the maneuvering to maintain the facade of rulership, and he was at last enabled to face the truth openly.

Shaul, then, symbolizes the tragedy of self- nullification. It is a soul-paralyzing state that thrusts one into a dream world of false values and renders the true challenges of life invisible. Grappling with guilt, taking responsibility – things that require courage, and without which repentance is out of the question – are within our reach only if we believe in ourselves as possessing the powers of those created in the Divine image.

# Shiur six

# Musar and 'Normality'

## PART 1

I₦ OUR LAST two *shiurim*, I have been rather argumentative. I thought it necessary, owing to the confusion that usually fogs the subject of humility. In moving on to our next topic, I am glad to return to a more reflective mode. Let me lead into this subject by referring back to our last discussion. We delved into a diagnosis of *ga'ava* (arrogance), the preoccupation with one's accomplishments and status vis-à-vis others. The search for such a diagnosis was motivated by an assumption that we took to be self-evident, namely, that *ga'ava* is a negative phenomenon – if you will, a moral pathology. Certainly, Chazal saw it that way.

But the world around us does not. In the marketplace of life, it is said, success belongs to him who blows his own horn. Reality seems to bear this out, at least in regard to the things that most readily define success for modern man – money, power, and prestige. Success-driven man (and this is the common species in our society) in turn assimilates a value system that not only sees no flaw in egocentricity, but sees it as a positive good. People today do not believe that one's conscience ought to flinch when indulging in self-praise or cultivating the good opinion of others. What we have called arrogance is commonly considered as man's natural instinct of self-preservation and self-interest. One who refrains from living as though he were the center of existence is acting in a strange, unnatural way, antithetical to man's true nature.

Here, then, is a challenge to the Musar orientation. Western man will never try to arrive at a workable definition of humility, because the whole idea is foreign to him. As a matter of fact, the instance of humility – a linchpin of Jewish ethics, as we have seen – exemplifies a larger predicament that besets the Jew who wants to actualize Torah without ghettoizing his lifestyle. This is the feeling that to take *tikkun* seriously means to be what the outside world would call 'maladjusted.' If we see ourselves as part of that world, something inside us is bound to share this assessment. What are we to do? Do we fight it, and try to live a 'normal' life in spite of everything? Or should we abandon all pretenses, resigning ourselves to an existence of incessant grappling and unrequited striving? Do we divorce ourselves from the accepted standards of normality in order to walk a path that runs counter to what is usually termed 'the pursuit of happiness?' The modern-day student of Musar ultimately must face these issues squarely.

I think this problem has two parts. Being adjusted, or living a normal life, can be discussed in relation to man vis-à-vis himself, connoting a state of freedom from anxiety, a psychological wholeness. Does Musar promise, value, or even make possible, such an existence? Secondly, we can ask whether we can achieve a well-adjusted existence with respect to the world around us. Is this possible, despite the value conflict? In this *shiur* we will concentrate on the first problem.

The following is an excerpt from *Madregat Ha-Adam*, written by a well-known figure in Musar circles, Rav Yosef-Yozl Horowitz of Novhardok (Novogrudok).[1] In it he claims that the goal of ethical living is *chayei menucha* – peaceful existence. But true peace, he believes, is a rather tempestuous affair:

> There is a peace that comes together with trials, as that pious man said [cited in *Chovot Ha-Levavot*], 'Even if You burn me with fire, it will only increase my love and joy in You,' because he feels a tranquility of soul and tremendous joy at the moment of the trial (*nisayon*). He doesn't call it a 'trial,' he calls it 'life.' For then he actualizes all

his powers, his courage, and his trust in God, and that is the point of living. The longer the trying situation lasts, or if [it ends but] is followed immediately by another one, he does not feel it a burden, an unfortunate occurrence which he cannot wait to be done with, but on the contrary, then all of his life-spirit is aroused, and then he feels alive on the path of wholeness. He is content to do battle with the *yetzer*.... There is no greater spirit of life than this, for his feeling is very high, and his mind is distilled and devoid of self-interest and passions. And when a man feels that he can fight [his] nature and win, according to his exalted outlook which is beyond the excitement of nature and all sensations and wants, this feeling gives him a tremendous pleasantness. As he continues to score victories in consecutive trials, his life-spirit will soar, and he will never entertain the thought of 'Better to forgo them along with their exaltation,' because trials and life are one and the same.

We will consider this description in the framework of our earlier study. The gap between human potential and its actualization is the backdrop of this passage. What kind of lifestyle is generated by an awareness of the gap? We are reading here of someone who is more than merely well adjusted. Rav Horowitz is thinking in terms of exhilaration. Doing battle with oneself and winning is the essence of life, and the seeker is likened to a warrior in constant pursuit of contest. At first glance, we may find this astounding: self- defeat resulting in soaring spirits? The answer, of course, is that Rav Horowitz does not think that the self that is defeated is the true self. A person possesses a higher self which is the true one. A fulfilled, peaceful existence means removing one's ego from the lower story and depositing it above. A man in relentless quest for *tikkun* constantly confronts his lower self, and is constantly actualizing potential.

To sum up, the polarity of 'what could be' as opposed to 'what is' generates an optimistic response, which is energized by the first of the two poles. The typical response is a heady delight in rising to the challenge. Rav Horowitz does not believe that a serious spiritual quest leads to personal maladjustment.

But it is clear that not all of our spiritual masters felt this way. Consider the following:

> It is well known that a man must be very careful to always be joyous and keep very distant from sadness …and even when he begins to examine himself and sees that there is nothing good in him, and he is full of sins, and the adversary [i.e., the evil inclination] wants to make him fall thereby into sadness and melancholy, Heaven forbid – even so he must not falter because of this, but rather he must seek and find within himself some small good. For how can it be that in all his life he has never done some mitzva or good deed? And even if, when he begins to look for that good thing, he sees that it too is full of wounds without an unblemished spot; that is to say, that it is full of selfish aims and strange thoughts and many other faults – but still, how could it be that there is not within that mitzva or good deed some small amount of good …for a man must search and seek to find within himself some small good to revive himself, in order to come to joy, as we mentioned above.

As you may have guessed, the foregoing was by Rav Nachman of Braslav (*Likutei Moharan* 282). Rav Nachman's disciples heard him stress that this teaching (or 'Torah,' in the Chasidic jargon) is one of the most basic and crucial tools of the religious person:

> Our master always cautioned us to walk with the above Torah, because it is a great foundation for anyone who wants to draw near to God, blessed be He, so as not to utterly lose his world. For most people who are far away from God, the main reason for their distance is melancholy and despair, because their spirits fall when they see in themselves the extent of the corruption in their actions – each one as he knows within himself the illnesses and pangs of his heart. And because of this, their spirits fall and most of them completely despair, and then they do not pray with any concentration at all, and they do not even do what they still could have done. Therefore, a man must internalize this fact: all these failures of the spirit, even though they are caused by evil deeds that he has truly done, yet the

despair and the sadness and the melancholy that befall him because of this are exclusively the work of the adversary, who is weakening his mind in order to defeat him completely, Heaven forbid. Therefore he must strengthen himself very much, to walk with this Torah, and to seek out and search within himself, every time, some small amount of good.

If we compare this to the picture painted by the 'Novhardoker', the difference in atmosphere is palpable. Gone are the invincible optimism, the ethical fearlessness. Here, the gap between what could be and what is leads to a lifestyle that is irresistibly drawn to agonizing confrontation with the latter. It seems that the tortured spirit here described can take no solace in the realization that he possesses great potential. What difference could that make, if actual life evidences only imperfection? No, theoretical pronouncements and subjective feelings about man's greatness, precisely because they are true, serve only to make the pain of missed chances and broken promises even less bearable. A sober appraisal of the state of affairs brings one to the brink of despair. Consolation can be had only through the search for good deeds actually done. That alone can prove that there is something to live for.

Rav Nachman seems to identify with this sensibility. He counsels that despite the anguished, torn existence that is the lot of religious man, there is no person whose life is without points of true, irrefutable light. Man's good deeds must be sought and discovered, their seeming insignificance notwithstanding, for it is their actuality that anchors the sense of purpose one needs to go on.

Rav Nachman, then, cannot even imagine what the Rav of Novhardok holds out as the attainable ideal of ethical life: *chayei menucha*, a 'peaceful existence.' It ought to be emphasized again, however, that the content of the peaceful existence of which Rav Horowitz speaks is a life of constant trial. A student of Musar is at peace, he would say, when spoiling for a fight. Rav Nachman, for his part, is far removed from any promise of inner harmony.

In the preceding citations, both Rav Horowitz and Rav Nachman of Braslav are talking to their disciples, but their teachings, of course, derived from their own personal experiences. Rav Kook, on the other hand, writes openly about himself in the following excerpt:[2]

> He who said of me that my soul is torn said well. Certainly, it is torn. We cannot imagine in our mind a man whose soul is not torn. Only the inanimate is whole, whereas man has contradictory ambitions, and there is constantly an inner battle within him. And the whole work of man is to unite the shreds in his soul through an embracing thought, in whose greatness and exaltedness all is included, and thus come to harmony.

A torn existence, says Rav Kook, is the norm for any thinking person (that is, one who is not 'inanimate'). However, he does view harmony as a desired goal. In part, this undoubtedly has to do with Rav Kook's mystical outlook, which views the human soul as a reflection of the cosmic unity. Practically speaking, the path to unity, according to Rav Kook, involves rising above the conflict. Exactly what this means is a lengthy matter on which we cannot dwell here. What we can derive from this self- description is that Rav Kook saw himself as a torn soul, and that harmony, for him, was a goal to work for but not something he thought he had achieved. Inner conflict is fundamental to the human condition, though it is a flaw that needs rectification.

Rav Soloveitchik was, like Rav Kook, aware of the pervasiveness of inner spiritual strife, but he had a different evaluation of this state of affairs. The following generalization is from his essay 'Majesty and Humility' (*Tradition*, Spring 1978, vol. 17, no. 2):

> Man is a dialectical being; an inner schism runs through his personality at every level.... the Judaic view posits that the schism is willed by God as the source of man's greatness and his election as a singular charismatic being. Man is great and creative because he is torn by conflict and is always in a state of ontological tenseness and perplexity. The fact that the creative gesture is associated with agony is a result of this contradiction, which pervades the whole personality of man....

The Psalmist proclaimed, 'I said in my haste all men are liars.' What kind of lie did the Psalmist have in mind when he hurled this serious accusation at man in general? Does man indeed engage constantly in immoral lying? By no means! The Psalmist is concerned with a different kind of lie – the existential lie that man tells, not others, but himself. Man is indeed a liar, because he is involved in an irresolvable contradiction, in an insoluble dialectic…. He swings like a pendulum between two poles: the thesis and the antithesis, the affirmation and the negation, identifying himself either with both of them or with neither. He must lie, but this inevitable lie is rooted in man's uniqueness and is a moral lie.

I would define the distinguishing feature of Rav Soloveitchik's position by referring to what I said earlier about what an 'adjusted' life means. I suggested two characteristics of such a life: freedom from anxiety and psychological wholeness. But here the schism within man is so central that the two characteristics must contradict each other. To live a life which is spiritually and psychologically whole, one must live simultaneously in differing, contradictory modes. This generates tension and anxiety. Freedom from anxiety is available, but only at the cost of psychological fragmentation. One must be willing to ignore one of the poles of existence, suppressing it from the realm of actuality and into the depths of oblivion, in order to achieve peace of mind. But in so doing, according to the Rav, one is cutting oneself off from the source of human creativity and greatness.

I should clarify that the rift within man, in Rav Soloveitchik's view, is not necessarily the one we have been emphasizing – spiritual potential versus actual life. Reading the article (recommended, of course) will reveal more about what he has in mind here. But the dual nature of man is a recurring and dominant motif in his writings and lectures, and was described by him in many ways and on different levels. The many facets of this are alluded to in the opening sentence of our excerpt.

Even without delving into Rav Soloveitchik's various works, it is easy to identify many conflicting aspects of human existence. To take a very partial inventory: rationality and emotionality as ways of life; rationality and irrationality as modes of thought; expressing individuality while being committed to society; career as opposed to family obligations. A Jewish existence has more conflicts to add: religious moral obligations stemming from different sources – the *Shulchan Arukh*, the 'spirit' of the Law, reason, conscience (they differ experientially even if they coalesce philosophically); universalism versus Jewish particularism, both on the level of principles and ideals, and on the level of personal identity (a potential source of very painful conflict). On all of these planes of existence, man feels his soul being tugged in opposite directions. He can respond to any of the conflicts by abdicating in favor of one side. His life will then be easier, and smaller. To be fully human, says Rav Soloveitchik, is to refuse to abdicate, to opt for the conflict, however agonizing.

I think we can gain some important insights on this subject by looking briefly at two more citations from the Rav, this time from his posthumously-published book *Worship of the Heart*, a work devoted to the subject of prayer. Towards the beginning of the book, Rav Soloveitchik elaborates considerably on the inner rift which rends our existence. The first quotation relates to a question which perhaps has been on your mind in the course of this discussion. Assume that I, for one, don't really experience life as an existential crisis, and seem to successfully lead a routine that runs along a well-oiled, snag-free course. Doesn't this in itself prove that the core-experience is meant to be harmonious? In the light of my own personal self-knowledge, wouldn't I be correct in concluding that a crisis-tossed existence is a sign of psychological maladjustment or worse? The following might be the Rav's response:

> The crisis is encountered in the strangeness of human destiny, of which man is not aware at all unless he is willing to acquaint himself with it. Such a crisis is not brought about by extraneous factors, or precipitated by coincidental entanglements…This type of crisis is searched out and discovered by man and accepted by him freely. It is not something which man tries to protect himself from, into

which man is dragged artificially because he is stupid and igno-
rant…Rather it is an experience of complete bankruptcy and failure
which stems from the deepest insight of man – as a great spiritual
personality.[3]

In other words, it is perfectly clear that one can go through life
without ever coming face-to-face with one's basic human inadequacy
and frustration. The decision to encounter oneself is a matter of free
choice, and therefore it cannot be forced on anyone. Yet Rav Soloveitchik steadfastly believes that Judaism wants to man to choose this pain
for himself, for therein lies human greatness.

The second insight I would like to glean is one which perhaps
"points the way". For getting back to my hypothetical self-description
as one who is far-removed from deep-seated crisis: Is there perhaps a
way of thinking, or a frame of mind, which I unconsciously adopt in
order to distance myself from pain? If such thinking could be identi-
fied, perhaps unmasking it (an act which may require courage) could
make Rav Soloveitchik's teaching on this matter practically relevant.
In this light let us examine the following:

> The reason for man's failure lies in the discrepancy between his
> creative fantasy and the objective means of self-fulfillment that are
> at his disposal. While his boundless fantasy expresses itself in ac-
> cents of endless desire and vast activity, the tools with which he tries
> to accomplish his goals are limited, since they belong to the finite
> order of things and forces. Man desires infinity itself yet must be
> satisfied with a restricted, bounded existence. When he reaches out,
> he anticipates the endless and boundless, enrapturing himself with
> the vision of unlimited opportunities. At the hour of achievement,
> however, he finds himself hemmed in by finitude.[4]

This passage reminded me of a mental experience that is shared by
more than a few yeshiva students. As a novice, the entering student
is awed by the vastness of Torah, as well as by the learning and the
spiritual stature of his mentors. At the beginning of the path, it is natural to feel excited at the prospect of emulating that level of spiritual

and scholarly achievement. But after a brief energizing start-up, the difficulty of it all – the intensive learning and the demands of a serious religious life – strikes home. Our student decides that if he wants to get anywhere, wisdom dictates the lowering of expectations, the setting of realistic goals, and being resigned to the fact that there are achievements that are out of reach. This pragmatic mind-set allows one to progress meaningfully without having to suffer frustration. But is there a price to pay for this blotting-out of frustration? What advice would Rav Soloveitchik have on this matter?

The content of this *shiur* touched on philosophical questions whose surface we have barely scratched. Our main aim has been to examine the issue from the point of view of Musar – how ought one to live. I hope that our study has served to open some avenues of thought. While it does not point to a single solution, it allows us to formulate the various considerations in retrospect, which is how I would like to conclude.

One issue we examined is whether a harmonious 'well-adjusted' life is possible for the Musar-oriented person; and if possible, is it realistically or only remotely so?

The further issue asks whether such a life is desirable. One reason for preferring a harmonious lifestyle would be the practical one. Certainly it is harder to live with conflict than without. This relative facility also has moral ramifications. More worthwhile things may be accomplished if each task is achieved in a smooth, non-turbulent manner that economizes our investment of time and emotional energy.

The larger question is whether either harmony or conflict can be held to be superior from a basic ethical standpoint. Unity may be preferred on the supposition that the ultimate spiritual reality of the world is a harmonious one. In this view, the very idea of inner spiritual conflict (analogous to interpersonal conflict) represents a flawed existence. This is the way we understood Rav Kook. On the other hand, we may view the conflict within man, along with Rav Soloveitchik, as a Divinely ordained fact of life that is a necessary vehicle of man's greatness. In this view, the aspiration to rid oneself of anxiety is equivalent to abdication of responsibility for the sake of comfort.

One further comment. My own sense is that, practically speaking, any serious student of Musar must be prepared for inner conflict. A person who has been so conditioned by the modern world that he will not take a single step that risks maladjustment will not get very far. Fear is what keeps us chained to our habits. Like an aspiring musician, we may aim for harmony as our final end; but all of our practice will be futile if we refuse to risk discord.

## Notes

1. The quotation is from the section entitled *Nekudat Ha-Emet*, chap. 4. Madregat Ha-Adam is the only complete volume penned by one of the major figures in Tenuat Ha-Musar, which strives to present a comprehensive approach to the subject.
2. *Chadarav,* personal writings of Rav Kook, compiled and edited by Ran Sarid, Mevaseret Tziyon, 1998, p. 115.
3. Rabbi J.B. Soloveitchik, Worship of the Heart, p. 31.
4. Ibid. p. 34.

# Shiur seven

# Musar and 'Normality'

## PART II

IN THIS *SHIUR* we will examine further the crucial question: Can one live in accordance with Jewish ethical standards and still be 'normal'? Our preceding lesson dealt with the reflexive aspect of this dilemma – living in an 'adjusted' manner vis-à-vis oneself. Now we will delve into the value conflict inherent in the very idea of living Jewishly in the modern world.

A large part of the strain on religious life in our times may be attributed to the perception that religion would prefer a world totally different from the one in which we live. One who believes that the values of the marketplace are totally at odds with the Torah values that command his inner conviction, but on the other hand lives a good part of his life according to the marketplace and its ways, is in a quandary that demands resolution. But what sort of resolution? We automatically think of various options that present themselves: psychological repression, abdication, compromise, resigning oneself to an alienated existence. Rather than mull over these unappealing choices, I would like to question the basic assumption of the dilemma. Are the values of the outside world truly at loggerheads with what a Torah life is meant to be? The answer we will suggest is negative. But a word of caution – our 'resolution' of the dilemma is not meant to dissolve the tension. We are looking for a point of view that will help us make our peace with a situation ridden with paradox.

I would like to follow the train of thought of a modern-day Orthodox Jewish thinker, Rabbi Sol Roth, who dealt with our problem extensively in *The Jewish Idea of Culture*. Rabbi Roth's point of departure is the dichotomy of *Torah u-madda*, which he translates as 'Torah and culture.' He advises us not to analyze these concepts merely as two thought-disciplines, for this would not expose their full human impact. We should first recognize that the two pursuits require two activities of differing existential significance:

> In the pursuit of cultural achievements, the human being experiences great ego-satisfaction. In the pursuit of Torah, an individual exhibits self-denial, i.e., he suppresses his own ego's inclinations in the interests of responding to the will of God. (p. 9)

In fact, the two concepts typify two life-attitudes that characterize and dominate human activity. Man can orient his activity in either a 'contractual' or a 'covenantal' mode. Contractual man is interested in self- realization. He operates socially and develops relationships mainly with the aim of furthering his personal goals. In this mode thrive the businessman cultivating his contacts and negotiating agreements, the student seeking the intellectual enrichment and stimulation offered by his teacher, and the artist painstakingly developing his creative technique through practice and study.

Covenantal man, on the other hand, rather than engaging the world for the sake of his own desired aims, does so for the sake of the relationships themselves. His commitment to a given relationship is not motivated by the desire to profit from it. His commitment is therefore unconditional, an end in itself. That is what makes it a covenant as opposed to a contract. We readily associate this experiential mode with the religious person who wants to serve God. But the same essential attitude is to be found in all types of service – be it a soldier who chooses to risk his life out of love for his country (rather than follow career interests), or a dedicated teacher or doctor who gives of himself for the good of others.

Of course, these two modes are not an either/or proposition. Human nature contains both of them. This duality is exemplified in something the Torah teaches about the marriage process. The Torah in two places exempts a newlywed from conscription. In the first (Devarim 20:5–7), the force that is preparing to go to battle is assembled and addressed:

> Who is the man who has built a house but has not yet dedicated it? Let him go and return home, lest he die in battle, and another man dedicate it…. And who is the man who has betrothed a woman but not yet married her? Let him go and return home, lest he die in battle, and another man marry her.

Further on (Devarim 24:5) we read:

> Should a man take a new wife, he will not go the army or be subject to any duty. He will be free for his home for one year, so that he may gladden the wife he has taken.

Why is this double exemption necessary? As our rabbis explain, each verse deals with a different stage in the two-tiered marriage process: betrothal (*erusin*) and marriage (*nisuin*). In the first instance, a soldier who is engaged is exempted to ensure that he does not die in battle. According to Chazal, the explicitly stated reason defines the scope of the exemption – this soldier does not fight, but he may be assigned safe military tasks. The second verse discusses a man who is already married – he is totally exempt for a year from any military service whatsoever, so that he will be 'free for his home.'

If we look more closely at the reasons for these laws, we notice an important distinction. The married man is freed in order to 'gladden his wife.' The betrothed man is exempt for a completely different reason. There, the Torah is not concerned with the welfare of the tragically widowed fiancée. She still has her life ahead of her, and can build her future with 'another man.' The calamity we seek to avert is the death of the first man before he has fulfilled his dream.

I believe that the basic difference between the two reasons illustrates the duality we have been discussing. A man who betroths a woman does not do so in order to 'gladden' her. He does not seek out a lonely person who is in need of a mate and offer her his hand in order to redeem her existence. On the contrary, he is seeking the life-partner who he believes will redeem *his own* loneliness, the person with whom he will be able to build the family and home of which he dreams. Despite all the romantic idealization we associate with courtship and betrothal, we are nevertheless discussing a contract, not a covenant.

But once we move on to the marriage itself, the Torah paints another picture. We expect the man to be concerned with something else – not fulfilling his own goals, but gladdening his wife. The essence of the marriage state is to forget oneself and be preoccupied with the welfare of the spouse. Once married, the relationship is transformed and becomes a covenant, in which the partners commit themselves to serve unconditionally. The enhancement and enrichment of the marriage relationship is an end in itself.

The distinction between covenantal and contractual life will help us deal with our original question: Is it true that the values of the outside world are opposed to those the Torah seeks to inculcate? The connection should be fairly clear. By and large, the values of modern society are those that dictate a contractual existence. Would it be accurate to say that the Torah denigrates such activity, and demands that we live wholly on a covenantal foundation of selfless commitment? I don't think so. Getting back to our example, the fact that the betrothed soldier is discharged so that his efforts not go unrewarded is an indication of the value Judaism sets on self-fulfillment.

Broadly stated, no one would ever get married or build a family if he were not acting out of self-interest. This is the very observation that caused our Sages, in Midrash Rabba, to interpret the verse 'And God saw everything that He had made, and it was very good' (Bereishit 1:31) with respect to the *yetzer ha-ra* (evil inclination): 'For were it not for the *yetzer ha-ra*, no man would build a house, take a wife, have children, or do business.' The Midrash is implying that what we call the evil inclination is in fact an essential aspect of humanity and is not necessarily evil – it depends on what you do with it. The physical development of the world and the propagation of the human race are morally good, and the means God ordained to achieve them are therefore called 'very good.'

Elsewhere Chazal elaborate on the moral importance of competitiveness, a trait that our 'saintly' side might tend to shrug off as sheer egotism. As shown in the following quotation from Midrash Tehilim 37, they detected a beneficial self-interest at work where we would least suspect: in the spiritual make-up of our father Avraham, the tower of *chesed* (loving-kindness).

> That is what Scripture says: 'Don't let your heart be jealous of sinners.' But of what should you be jealous? 'Of the fear of God all the day' (Mishlei 23).... And when was Avraham jealous? When he said to Malkizedek [whom the Rabbis identify as Shem the son of Noach], 'In what merit did you go out of the Ark?' He said to him, 'Because of the charity that we did.' He said to him, 'What charity was there for you to do? Do you mean to say that there were poor people then? The only people there were Noach and his sons!' ...He said to him, 'We did charity with the animals and birds. All night, instead of sleeping, we gave food to this one and that one.' ...Avraham then said to himself, 'If giving charity to animals and birds was enough to merit their escape from the Ark ...then if I were to do charity with human beings, who are created in the image of angels, how much more so would I merit being saved from all harm!' Whereupon 'Avraham planted a tree (*eshel*)' (Bereishit 21) [*eshel* is taken as an acronym for *akhila, shetiya, livaya*, 'eating, drinking and accompanying']; that is, he practiced hospitality. That is why Shlomo said, 'I have seen that all labor and industrious activity are nothing more than one man's jealousy of another' (Kohelet 4).

In truth, we are not doing justice to the contractual side of our personality if we view it as an ethical embarrassment. Were we to live only as covenantal beings, we would lack a whole array of characteristics that are necessary for creative endeavor. Industriousness, willpower, mental acumen, and competitiveness are all traits that have moral significance. Yeshiva students are encouraged to develop these traits in the interest of Torah study (a spiritual value!). Think of a society that rests on its laurels, and does not invest effort and means in constantly improving its economic, social, and military standards. Such a society, besides setbacks in the above-mentioned areas, is probably also suffering moral degeneration: increased laziness, pleasure-seeking, irresponsibility. The torpor that beset the Israeli army before the Yom Kippur War was a moral failure, besides being potentially catastrophic militarily.

At the same time, it is clear that experientially, industriousness and competitiveness are totally different from the covenantal traits of self-sacrifice and commitment. The first set of values derives from the secular world; the second set derives from the transcendent – these are the values that compel man to transcend himself and reach out to what is beyond him. Here again we face an inner rift of the type we saw in the preceding lesson. Accommodating these two different mind-sets is a uniquely human task; dealing squarely with this tension is what makes a person whole.

If we stop the discussion here, and return to our original question – are the values of the marketplace opposed to Torah values? – we may say that the religious Jew need feel no strangeness when carrying on the routine of life in secular society. The ways of the modern world represent valid and desirable aims from the religious standpoint. We would appear to have allayed the antagonism between Jewish life and the society around us, and to remain (as we concluded in the previous *shiur*) with the challenge of the tension within religious life itself.

Personally, I believe that this somewhat satisfying conclusion is valuable. At the same time, I would be dishonest if I left it at that. The value-conflict with the modern world is still there, and trying to evade the issue will not do. In our next *shiur* we will look at some of the reasons why, despite the Torah's acknowledgment of the importance of the secular creative impulse, the Musar-oriented Jew can expect difficulty in looking for a home in the twenty-first century.

# Shiur eight

# Musar and 'Normality'

## PART III

In the preceding discussion, we analyzed some of the materialistic values of modern society and discovered, perhaps to the surprise of our religious instincts, their great moral significance. We gave these principles their due, with the help of Rabbi Roth, categorizing them as contractual values, as opposed to the covenantal values that typify religious life as such. Yet all this does not make normality readily accessible to us. Alienation is an ever-present problem for one who would live his life according to Torah ethics. Our appreciation of the secular world enables us to play a role in it, productively and even enthusiastically; but the sense of being an outsider persists. Why is this so?

Primarily because, while we come to the modern world recognizing the validity of its value system, society does not mutually reciprocate. It is not merely the fact that the covenantal aspect to humanness is denied in the modern world, though this would be bad enough. The dismal truth is that the vacuum left by the absence of covenantal values is actually usurped by the secular society. The goals of self-realization, personal achievement, and creativity, along with their corollaries, become magnified out of all proportion. The marketplace sees them as the be-all and end-all of humanity and demands that they be accorded absolute fealty. The Musar approach to life can never identify with this proposition. Contractual ideals untempered and unfettered become grotesque caricatures of themselves.

As an example, let us consider *tzedek* (justice). This ideal has nothing to do with altruism, and is a contractual virtue. The aim of justice is to guard the rights of the individual; its practical application is achieved in courts of law where rival parties defend their respective interests. Needless to say, the Torah agrees that justice is of paramount importance and is practiced by God Himself. But even such a cardinal concept suffers from the excesses of the secular society. A case in point is the theory espoused by Israeli Chief Justice Aharon Barak, one of the world's foremost jurists. In his view, no human activity can be legally neutral. He writes:

> All human behavior is subject to judicial regulation. Even when a certain type of activity – such as friendly relations or subjective thought – is governed by the autonomy of the individual will, this autonomy exists because it is recognized by the law. Without such recognition, anyone would have the right to invade this area (i.e., private autonomy).[1]

In the same article, Professor Barak coined his famous motto: 'In my view, the whole earth is full of the law (*melo kol ha-aretz mishpat*).' The presumptuousness of this approach is apparent when we note that the source of Barak's idiom is a verse in Yeshayahu 6 that refers to the Divine Glory. This philosophy is given practical application in the legal activism whereby the Israeli Supreme Court uses the judicial apparatus to decide issues that appear to have nothing to do with law.[2]

The human mind, it would seem, abhors an ideological vacuum. When transcendence per se is denied, pervasive secularism intrudes into the empty space and takes over. The natural tendency is for people to become 'true believers' in the area of their interest (professional or otherwise), thus granting profound existential significance to ideas such as law, democracy, and the free press, which to a religious mind signify no less – but no more – than *yishuvo shel olam*, furthering civilization.

Thus it is that when a conscientious Jew joins society at large in its worthwhile pursuits, and affirms its moral commitment to the freedom of the individual and his right to a fulfilled existence, a part of him is brooding. He feels the tug of his allegiance to a wholly different set of values that have nothing to do with the pursuit of happiness, an array of concepts that he cannot communicate to his fellows at the economic exchange.

From this alienated vantage-point, the thoughtful religious person becomes sensitized to the various ways in which contractual man appropriates the halo of supposed transcendence. Let us exploit our 'outsider' status for a few critical glimpses.

Dr. Daniel Shalit is a penetrating observer of modern dilemmas. In a noteworthy insight, he finds these dilemmas mirrored in the artificial, all-encompassing environments in which we spend so much of our time. The following is from his essay 'Shopping-Mall Man.'³

The Mall presents before our very eyes, essentially and tangibly, the entire culture of our times. First of all, it is entirely detached from nature – separated from the ground by thousands of square meters of cement, basements, shelters, and parking lots. Second, it is detached from Heaven as well – covered by a gigantic plastic dome. And between the cement and the plastic – a whole man-made world. Everything – sidewalks and stores, waterfalls and ponds, plants and trees, all that the senses absorb – the colors we see, sounds we hear, smells, humidity, temperature, and of course the walkways, the stairs, the angles – all planned, controlled, and computerized to the last detail. And all so beautiful, so efficient, so brilliant: the victory of man....

One might think that man would strive to get out, to connect up with what is beyond the Mall – with the transcendent. But no: the movement is, for the time being, not going out, but to bring *in* everything that is *outside*. Within this so-human creation, the Mall, man builds his own nature and his own super- nature, an Earth and a Heaven...Would you like nature? Here you are – ponds, plants, bushes, animals. Something beyond nature? Put on the three-dimensional stereophonic video-mask, and you can fly in the expanses of space, travel back and forth in time, participate in space-battles and dragon wars. And fantastic movies are only the tip of the iceberg. The Mall has become a whole empire of fantasy. What is sold are mainly 'thrill-packages' and not physical objects. For even physical objects – soap, trousers, and surely cars – are sold, as the ad men have discovered, not for their practical value, but for the dream, the experience that they give to the consumer.

In the perspective of what we have already discussed, the shopping mall is a concrete expression (*double-entendre* intended) of the demand of the modern marketplace to be total, ultimate. It asserts that it can satisfy man's yearning for the truth which is beyond his senses, adapting itself, on the one hand, and maneuvering the human mind, on the other, to the point where every conceivable need is met within its confines. The denizens of the Mall are blissfully unaware of their pathetic situation. But ought an outsider be jealous of such normality?

Shalit finds that the trend is buttressed by the direction taken by modern science.[4]

The same thing that manifests itself tangibly in the marketplace happens more abstractly in science and technology. Physics, that factual, unemotional, and exact science, has long since turned into fantasy. You can find among today's physical terms magic and strangeness, not to mention quarks and quasars, black holes and the secrets of cosmology. Physics today is itself science fiction.... Man set out to discover the laws of matter, and ended up unwillingly discovering a kind of spiritual world.... Likewise in technology – man set out to build cranes, gears, and steam engines, and found himself in the world of programs, communications, and information, a world that is essentially spiritual.... Even commerce is no longer barter of needed goods, not even trade in currency, but primarily transfers and directives, arrangements and agreements – all of them 'intelligent,' nonmaterial activities. Does anyone have money? Silver bars? Copper coins? We hardly even have paper money – we have credit cards, standing orders, understandings, and banking arrangements.

These fascinating developments once again address, and tantalize, the human striving for the beyond. And here again, it is all an illusion. Dr. Shalit goes on to state what should be obvious. True, the concepts of modern physics – energy, magnetic fields, forces, electromagnetic waves – are not as grossly physical as weight, size, and distance. But they are still physical, because they occur in space-time and can be observed by all. They are totally different from even the simplest spiritual experiences – pain, guilt, love – which are personal and subjective, and nevertheless real. But modern man is blind to the distinction; therein lies the danger.

> As long as matter was coarse, as long as the machines were metallic bodies, and smokestacks polluted the heavens, it was obvious that man has something that is beyond the mechanical, and that he must strive for the beyond. But now, when the mechanics have become ethereal and subtle, the need is no longer self-evident. It is not easy to explain to someone why the memory and the thought process of the computer are essentially different from human memory and thought, why the computer's speech and 'intelligence' are not even the faintest shadow of real speech and intelligence, why music and drawings created by a computer are dead, no matter how perfect. And so grows a whole generation that knows nothing about real speech, real intelligence and inspired music, and all it has is repressed, ill-defined distress.[5]

The foregoing observations focus on recent realities. In the early 1960s, Rav Soloveitchik noted another variation on our theme. In 'The Lonely Man of Faith,' he distinguishes typologically between Adam the first and Adam the second, an archetypical division that parallels Rabbi Roth's distinction between contractual man and covenantal man. (Rabbi Roth's thinking is in fact heavily influenced by Rav Soloveitchik's writings.) He claims that Adam the first, the 'majestic man' of accomplishment and creativity, has undergone a transformation in our time.

> Majestic Adam has developed a demonic quality; laying claim to unlimited power – alas, to infinity itself.... I am not referring here to man's daring experiments in space. From a religious point of view ...they are quite legitimate and in compliance with the divine testament given to Adam the first that he should rule nature. When I say that modern man is projecting a demonic image, I am thinking of man's attempt to dominate himself, or to be more precise, of Adam the first's desire to identify himself with the total human personality, declaring his creative talents as ultimate, ignoring completely Adam the second and his preoccupation with the unique and strange transcendental experience....
>
> The desire for total domination colors Majestic Adam's attitude even when he practices religion. He, of course, comes to a place of worship. He attends lectures on religion and appreciates the ceremonial, yet he is searching not for faith ...but for religious culture. He seeks not the greatness found in sacrificial action but the convenience one discovers in a comfortable, serene state of mind. He is desirous of an aesthetic experience rather than a covenantal one, of a social ethos rather than a divine imperative.... he is not yet ready for a genuine faith experience which requires the giving of one's self unreservedly to God, who demands unconditional commitment, sacrificial action, and retreat. Western man diabolically insists on being successful. Alas, he wants to be successful even in his adventure with God. If he gives of himself to God, he expects reciprocity. He also reaches a covenant with God, but this covenant is a mercantile one. In a primitive manner, he wants to trade 'favors' and exchange goods. The gesture of faith for him is a give-and-take affair.

This is another way of seeing the secular intrusion into the realm of the transcendent. Dr. Shalit pointed out this tendency in relation to the modern creation of an alternative, bogus spirituality. The Rav, on the other hand, documents the exploitation of existing modes of faith-expression as being subject to man's self-interest. Contractual man comes even to his encounter with the truly transcendent, equipped only with his bartering, tradesman's mind-set.

This brings us to the close of our examination of whether maintaining twenty-first-century 'normality' is inimical to the serious practice of Musar. To speak in general terms, I think that the brunt of the material and observations we have seen appears to preclude a whole- hearted declaration of compatibility. A more precise answer is something that each person must give himself. But I will say a bit more about my own feelings on the matter.

It seems to me that while a certain degree of alienation is unavoidable, the unpleasantness is compounded if we feel our religious moorings threatened by the totality of the modern experience. Without ignoring the dangers that Western society presents, we can view ourselves as a corrective to it, rather than as a species threatened by it. The modern world started out with some good, beneficial, moral ideas and insights. It went awry by taking things to unfortunate excess. Perhaps by maintaining our ties to the society in which we live, our own personal improvement will be a step toward the restoration of saner proportions in the world of values.

Our discussions are about to change their focus. Until now we have been discussing problems of ideology; now we must deal with psychology. The prospect of motivated change and human growth, which our endeavor assumes possible, arouses serious questions. Most obviously, how is such change accomplished? One intuitively feels that intellectual study alone is insufficient. But beyond this, we must investigate how the modern environment influences the capacity to change. As we will see, there are important factors that make change more difficult today than it was in the past.

It would be fitting to introduce this topic with another quotation from the closing passage of 'The Lonely Man of Faith.'

Modern Adam the second ...finds himself lonely, forsaken, misunderstood, at times even ridiculed by Adam the first, by himself. When the hour of estrangement strikes, the ordeal of the man of faith begins, and he starts his withdrawal from society, from Adam the first – be he an outsider, be he himself. He returns, like Moses of old, to his solitary hiding and to the abode of loneliness.

The Rav says that Adam the second finds himself estranged from Adam the first, *who may very well be himself.* An individual Jew may find himself identifying with the transcendent goals of the man of faith, and at the next moment – having assimilated Adam the first's drive for dominion – may ridicule and fail to understand those same goals. Now the arena of the struggle, even its very definition, is changed. It is no longer an ideological grappling with a callous rival, but a psychological wrestling with oneself. We will try to take a closer look at the nature of this duel, its strategies and tactics.

### Notes

1. *Iyunei Mishpat*, no. 17 (5752), p. 477.
2. Such as whether there can be a women's minyan at the Kotel Ha-Ma'aravi. It is instructive to note that even in Torah legislation, the assumption is that anything not specifically prohibited by the Torah is permitted, and belongs to the legally neutral domain (*heter*). A verse like 'You shall eat any pure bird' is judged superfluous and incomprehensible by the Halakha unless understood as an oblique reference to the prohibition of eating impure birds. Cf. Rambam's *Sefer Ha-Mitzvot*, positive commandments 149–152.
3. D. Shalit, *Sichot Penim, Jerusalem 5755, pp. 103–107.*
4. Ibid. p. 107.
5. Ibid. pp. 110–111.

# Shiur nine

# The Dynamics of Growth

## PART I

THE PRACTICAL AIM of Musar is to achieve personal growth and change. Of course, these are processes that 'happen' to everyone during his or her lifetime. But in Musar, we strive to determine the direction and actively influence the outcome. How is this to be accomplished? Certainly, the issue of practical methodology must be considered. But I think it advisable not to jump straightaway into specific educational approaches, for I believe that our efforts will be more fruitful if we succeed in first clarifying the objective.

This is particularly the case in the present day and age, when the objective needs to be defined in terms that differ from those which sufficed in previous generations. I am not implying that the classical ethical ideals are no longer appropriate, but rather that the obstacles to change in the modern world are substantially different and more formidable. We need not only to know where we would like to go, but to be aware of what must be overcome on the way.

## Musar in the Metropolis

The proposition that a person can change himself for the better implies that that he has a measure of control over himself. Of course, when it comes to specific actions, we perhaps have little trouble accepting the soundness of the principle of free will, a fundamental component of the Jewish outlook. But what about changing not only one's deeds but oneself? Do we have control there, too, or are we being buffeted by the aggressive forces of the environment? Consider the following:

> Man is a differentiating creature. His mind is stimulated by the difference between a momentary impression and the one that preceded it. Lasting impressions, impressions which differ only slightly from one another, impressions which take a regular and habitual course and show regular and habitual contrasts – all these use up, so to speak, less consciousness than does the rapid crowding of images, the sharp discontinuity in the grasp of a single glance, and the unexpectedness of onrushing impressions. These are the psychological conditions which the metropolis creates. With each crossing of the street, with the tempo and multiplicity of economic, occupational, and social life, the city sets up a deep contrast with small-town and rural life with reference to the sensory foundations of psychic life…. [In rural settings] the rhythm of life and sensory mental imagery flows more slowly, more habitually, and more evenly.

Thus did the sociologist Georg Simmel[1] describe the psychic reality facing urban man at the outset of the twentieth century. Human living means interaction with one's surroundings. The demands of the metropolis, the preeminent habitat of modern man, are more sharply pressing than those of rural life. But as Simmel goes on to describe, the difference is not merely quantitative. City living requires the development of a psychological mechanism without which survival would be precarious, but whose constant activation tends to paralyze a good part of our emotional makeup.

Why is this so? It is because life in the rural setting is played out in the deeper regions of the personality, the home of the emotional attachments and meaningful interpersonal relations. If we were to try to live "from the heart" in the rapidfire metropolitan environment, our psyche would be subjected to unbearable pressure. It is for this reason that in the city, the intellect must take control. As Simmel concludes:

Thus the metropolitan type of man ...develops an organ, which protects him from the threatening currents and discrepancies of his external environment which would uproot him. He reacts with his head instead of his heart.... The reaction to metropolitan phenomena is shifted to that organ which is least sensitive and quite remote from the depth of the personality.

Simmel wrote this at a time when there still were places to live in that were not cities. Today, for the most part, this situation no longer exists. The same unabated flow of information, of advertising, of attempts to direct and divert our attention, today characterizes most corners of the globe. Moreover, the sources of the bombardment are no longer the immediate metropolitan environment. Technology has made our minds prey to incessant intrusions from virtually everywhere in the world.

Because of this, our emotional selves tend to become deadened. Our interaction with the environment becomes superficial and intellectualized. Were we to react humanly to every event, to attempt to tie all the rapid-fire events to our existential being, we would go insane. Our only option is to condition ourselves to live with our nimble, clever minds, ignoring our deeper selves to the point where we can go on sipping our coffee while watching the most calamitous news reports.

The implications for spiritual growth can be readily seen. The locus of growth is the whole person. Much like any living organism, human growth thrives on stability, and is harmed by upheaval and rupture. In a nonconducive environment, it becomes too risky to take up residence in the basic, inner chambers of our personality. Yet our conscious goals and awareness can hardly affect our emotional foundations if we live in a way that leaves those foundations psychologically off- limits. This realization calls for a reassessment of one's lifestyle. One could seriously consider reducing electronic consumption, allotting time for quiet hours, seeking out more secluded surroundings (yeshiva, country, etc.).

## Is There a *Yetzer Tov*?

The complexity of our efforts to practice Musar is compounded by another feature of our times. This second factor, like the first, is related to the psychological makeup of modern man, but the problem here is not a result of the urban lifestyle, but of a truncated emotional stereotype that has become endemic to our time.

A noted Israeli religious thinker and educator, Yitzchak Raphael Etzion, contrasts the religious man with the nonbeliever in terms of their inner 'workings.' He claims that in either case, world-outlook is determined primarily not by reason, but by needs and preferences. The following is from the concluding section of 'The Psychology of Heresy and Faith.'

In section 1 of this article I concluded that the psychological basis of nonbelief in God is the glorification of man, that is, the belief in man's omnipotence. This faith satisfies man's arrogance, his psychological need to view himself as the greatest of creatures. But from the other sections of this article it may be concluded that belief in God, as well, satisfies the same psychological need, for this belief includes (among its long-range corollaries) the following principles: that man is the only living creature (1) who has free will, (2) whose soul is eternal, (3) to whom the Creator revealed Himself and charged with various tasks. It follows that both faith and heresy satisfy the very same need of man – the need to hold himself in esteem above the other creatures. The question then is: What are the factors that produce such diametrically opposed ways of satisfying the same need in the believer and the nonbeliever?

On the basis of the preceding sections, we may reason that the difference is that the nonbeliever, that is, he who believes in man's omnipotence, sets a higher value on the *immediate* results of his belief, whereas one who believes in God considers the *long-range* results of his belief to be more important.

This is seen in the following psychological phenomena:

1. To the nonbeliever, the present and the near future are more important, whereas to the believer, the distant future is more im-

portant. The first says, so to speak, 'Eat and drink, for tomorrow we die,' and after death there is nothing. But the second is concerned with what will be after death.

2. The believer in man's omnipotence, who denies God, is enraptured with the feeling of great freedom, that his belief grants him in an *immediate* way, for 'who is his master'?[2] And even if his belief in natural law brings him to determinism and the assumption that man has no free will, he does not see this as belittling his own worth, because the same is true of all men. But the believer in God is not satisfied with the feeling that he himself is no lower than other men. He cannot make peace with the belittling of *humanity in general*, which is the upshot of placing man alongside all the beasts and inanimate objects that have no free will.[3]

Dr. Etzion goes on to demonstrate this distinction in other ways, but I think the idea is sufficiently clear. Both types, the believer and the nonbeliever, are responding to the instinctive feeling of man's unique stature. But one thinks that man's superiority signifies mainly his birthright to live as an uninhibited, self- glorifying despot – a view that requires the removal of God from the universe. The other translates man's uniqueness into the power to achieve moral greatness, a power that comes from God, on the one hand, and makes one responsible to God, and requires man's life-long effort to realize, on the other. The non believer is motivated by the need for immediate gratification. The believer's needs have a more far- reaching, long-range character. He is concerned with life after death. He is not exhilarated by a feeling of freedom, which profound analysis exposes as the mere self- delusion of a cog in the cosmic causal chain.

It follows that a personality habituated to immediate gratification, whose repertoire of needs does not include any that are based on thoughtful analysis of man's place and role in the world, will find itself inclining towards 'heresy'. The last word was deliberately put in quotation marks. One does not have to profess heresy intellectually in order to feel like a heretic, or to live like one. The goal of Musar can be said to be the constant, progressive banishment of heresy from all aspects of our life. It is not enough to believe in the importance of spirituality. One must possess the requisite psychological workings, the inner structure that incorporates the inclination to morality, the *need* for a higher lifestyle.

Here modern man is at a distinct disadvantage, because the dominant trends in classical psychological theory have dealt a serious blow to the possibility of developing such inclinations. The following excerpt from an essay by Prof. Reuven Feuerstein, a psychologist, and Rav Raphael Feuerstein, the chairman of the International Center for the Improvement of Learning Skills, explains the background of this state of affairs. The authors describe a debate regarding the origin of man's moral nature.

> We would like to distinguish between the conceptions that assume continuity in the development of moral judgment and needs, from the primary levels to the more developed, which we will call the 'consecutive approach'; and those conceptions which we will call the 'non consecutive approach' (which we ourselves will represent), that assume that moral judgment and needs are created in a manner quite detached from the primary levels.
>
> Freud stands out as representing the consecutive approach. A group of theories that originate with Freud argues that the moral needs of the mature adult are an outgrowth of the system of primary needs (the id). The primary needs, dominated by the pleasure principle, are transformed by several mechanisms, one of which is 'sublimation' ... [but] the primary needs still activate the needs that are more progressive and developed.
>
> To illustrate this point: A man walking on the street sees a house ablaze. From within are heard cries for help. The man runs with all his strength, leaps up the stairs, and breaks down the front door. He locates the cries for help in an inner room of the burning house, runs through the flames oblivious to the danger to himself, and rescues a child from the burning room. According to Freud and his followers, the supremely moral behavior of the rescuer is a product of the primary needs themselves. It is just that these needs

undergo a set of transformations until the moral needs are created. It
is like the primary motion of the piston in the motor of a car, which
through complex systems of gears, ultimately causes the rotation of
the wheels of the car.

As opposed to the 'consecutive' theories, the theory of mediated
learning of Feuerstein argues (as does the theory of Wygotzky) that
man's more developed thought structures, as well as his complex
(as opposed to primary) needs, do not come from primary thought
structures and needs that have developed continuously. Rather,
they originate in learning processes generated by society.... They
are not an extension of the primary-primitive structures, but a
developmental leap.[4]

Of the two theories on the nature of moral needs, the Freudian
view has had the undeniably greater impact on the modern psyche.
But undeniable as well is the fact that the second view is the one
rooted in the outlook of Chazal. It is difficult to conceive the world of
traditional Jewish ethics in any other way. The Rabbis expounded in
Midrash Rabba on Kohelet 4:13, 'A miserable but wise child is better
than an old, foolish king:'

> 'A miserable but wise child' – that is the *yetzer tov* [good inclination].
> Why is he [i.e., the *yetzer tov*] called a child? Because he doesn't
> meet up with a man until the age of thirteen. And why is he called
> miserable? Because most people don't listen to him. And why is he
> called wise? Because he teaches people the straight path. '…is better
> than an old, foolish king' – that is the *yetzer ha-ra* [evil inclination].
> Why does Scripture call him a king? Because everyone listens to him.
> And why does it call him old? Because he is with man from child-
> hood through old age. And why does it call him foolish? Because
> he teaches man the way of evil.

Chazal were not psychologists in the modern sense, but they were
sensitive educators with profound human understanding. They held
that the *yetzer tov,* the *inclination* to do good, is a fundamentally distinct stage of development, which can take hold only in adolescence.

It is a need that is totally independent of the primitive *yetzer ha-ra*, though conflicts there may be. Chazal would certainly agree that the evil inclination can and must be sublimated (see the discussion of contractual values in the preceding studies ). On the other hand, they steadfastly affirmed that the inclination to do good is a separate psychological and spiritual faculty, which needs to function and be cultivated in its own right.

But modern man, having convinced himself that he is dominated by primary, subterranean urges that cannot be escaped, dooms himself to the retarded moral development at the root of the baseness of the popular culture. I hope that in our next *shiur* we will see more clearly why this is so. Awareness of the harmful effects of this warped self-image will serve to underscore the necessity of overcoming it.

To sum up, we noted two problems that make Musar a more difficult assignment in the present age than previously. The first is the perpetual bombardment of ideas, situations, and information that devour our attention and emotional resources, impairing our capacity to grow. The second, which we will continue to analyze in the next *shiur*, is the denial of the *yetzer tov* as an independent component of the human psyche. In closing, I would add that although these two considerations truly make Musar more difficult, they also make it more necessary.

## Notes

1. In *The Metropolis and Mental Life,* chap. 2, as quoted in *Man Alone, Alienation in Modern Society,* ed. Eric and Mary Josephson, pp. 152–153.
2. Psalms, chap. 12, 5.
3. In *IyunimBi-Vaayot Emuna* [Studies on Issues of Faith] (Kfar Chabad: Yad Ha-Chamisha Press, 1969), pp. 66–68.
4. 'The Crisis in Education Toward Jewish Values Through the Spectrum of the Theory of Mediated Learning,' in *Likutei Shoshanim: Anthology in Memory of Shoshana Lasker (Hebrew),* ed. Dr. Yossi Green, 5760 (2000).

# Shiur ten

# Dynamics of Growth

## PART II

In OUR LAST *shiur* we noted that Chazal's insistence on the reality of the *yetzer tov* runs counter to a mainstream view in modern psychology, that morality exists in man because his primary instinctive needs undergo various modes of transformation, ultimately expressing themselves as moral behavior. Yet we haven't yet dealt fully with the question: what difference does this make?

The answer becomes clear when we consider the internal significance of the moral demands implicit in Torah ethics, as opposed to the more primary human activities.[1] Take, for example, a person who eats to satisfy his hunger. The connection between eating and the desired result is simple; acting it out requires nothing more than instinctive action. On the other hand, religious action requires the fulfillment of a *mitzva* because of the Divine imperative. This is a major intellectual effort, and assumes a relatively advanced level of emotional development and maturity. It requires consciousness of one's place in the world vis-à-vis the Creator, belief in man's purpose in life, and identification with the ideal that the mitzva represents. Intelligent perception of the framework in which I live (family, society, the world) creates awareness and needs of an order totally different from my basic instincts. It generates the need to be held accountable, the need for responsibility, for the fulfillment of expectations of oneself, and for redemption. These are inclinations based on intelligence. The inclinations of the nonbeliever are based more on instinct.

The world of Jewish ethics, as projected by our sources, makes no sense on the assumption that egotism is man's only option. Modern man perceives correctly that 'sublimated' self-interest can never explain the heights of idealism and self-sacrifice that are the goal of Musar, and chooses to ignore the reality that such 'incomprehensible' heights have indeed been demonstrated in Jewish history, and, for that matter, in world history. He opts for the easy way out, and interprets his life as a succession of gratifications interrupted by the efforts to attain them. The result is stunted spiritual growth. Any discussion of ethical ascent falls on deaf ears because of the lack of the emotional apparatus necessary to absorb it meaningfully. The result of this is the glaring disparity – apparent to all – between man's intellectual and technological prowess, on the one hand, and the primitiveness of popular culture, on the other.

Can the typical person of our time make sense of the following passage from Rav Kook (*Musar Avikha*, introduction, pt. 3)?

> Prayer is an important indicator through which one may know if he is really purifying his heart, as his Creator, blessed be He, desires. Therefore one must take great care not to be drawn by his own desire for physical pleasures, such as food and drink, because then physical nature will be ingrained in him so that he will not feel that he is missing the true, sacred things, and then he will forfeit prayer, which is basic to service of God. For if he comforts himself with being to able to eat and be satisfied and other such vanities, he cannot imagine, when he says the Aleinu prayer, that the world will be perfected in the kingdom of God and the idols will be destroyed and the wicked will turn to God, because what harm can idols do to one whose heart and eyes are given over to filling his stomach with delicacies?

Rav Kook means what he says. The statement quoted above was written as a practical guideline.

## An Educational Debate

In recent years, religious educators have been struggling to counter the tidal wave of individualism that has engulfed our generation. Among some of them I find a trend, which concerns me greatly, toward excessive *limud zekhut*, furnishing an ideological justification for the current state of spiritual infantile paralysis that I described above. They assume individualism to be a spiritual boon, and see the necessity of adapting to the new generation's outlook as an asset. Here is what Rav Elisha Aviner says of the current preoccupation with the self:

> In the past, the cultivation of inner spiritual selfhood was the pre-
> serve of our spiritual giants.... Rav Kook testifies that he himself
> took this path: 'I am always searching for what is within my own soul.'
> This path, which in the past was reserved only for special people, is
> now demanded of the masses. What caused the change? Based on a
> principle mentioned by Rav Kook in several places ...we can explain
> that the change has been caused by the ascent (i.e., spiritual progress)
> of the masses. In the past, people in general contented themselves
> with disciplined allegiance to the values with which the leaders of
> the generation charged them, and with loyalty to traditional ideals.
> Their 'I' achieved hardly any expression, because of its weakness and
> superficiality. Man was insufficiently enlightened and unaccustomed
> to advanced moral feelings. For this reason, self-actualization might
> have aroused the animal within him. For the sake of their spiritual
> upbringing, the masses were told to forgo the 'I,' nullify themselves
> at the feet of great individuals, and put into practice the values that
> were placed before them. But the accelerated cultural progress of
> mankind has caused a change in the human consciousness as well,
> especially in regard to awareness of the self. What in the past was a
> vital need of special individuals is now the necessity of the many.[2]

In fairness, the foregoing is excerpted from a rather lengthy presentation. But all the same, it expresses a quite common and, with all due respect, incorrect (to my mind) assessment of our current situation.

What further disturbs me, however, is that even educators who do not concur with the above opinion seem to have been influenced by the prevailing conception of human nature. Here, for example, is part of a presentation that takes issue with Rav Aviner. Rav Eliezer Scheinwald has a less idealized attitude toward self-realization:

> Self-realization is a cultural trend that directs all personal resources toward maximal personal success (as opposed to the advancement of society), personal status, and higher professional and economic achievement. These will supposedly attain for the individual pleasure, satisfaction, and a sense of fulfillment. The term 'self-realization' is misleading because it includes the word 'self' (*atzmi*), which in Hebrew also connotes spiritual uniqueness, the aim of actualizing the profound, spiritual core of the personality. Self-realization, on the other hand, is about needs …and the sources of personal motivation – the drive for success.[3]

On the one hand, I certainly identify with this more realistic analysis of the vogue of obsessive self- realization. But I hope I won't be considered picayune for taking one of the formulations here to heart. In the passage, self-realization is connected with needs, motivation, and drives. This leaves the impression that aims unconnected with self-realization aren't needs. Rather, they are chafing, externally imposed tasks, in the spirit of Rav Aviner's description ("forgoing the 'I'"). I think it important for us to be very clear on this point. Our aim is for the individual to *live* the need for service to others, to loathe the prospect of a life experientially concerned only with the next meal or the next million dollars, to feel within himself the greatness – and the smallness – implied by the Divine imperative to man. The need for higher living is not only to be objectively assessed, but subjectively experienced. Our claim is that *this* is human nature.

Hence, I would agree more with the formulation of Rav Yaakov Ariel:

> The Divine command does not stand outside of man, and is not

opposed to human conscience. On the contrary, the human conscience is a copy and internalization of the absolute eternal Divine....
When we say that the educator has an obligation to educate, we do
not mean that the command is forced upon him and the student
from without. It is autonomous. Both the educator and the pupil
have souls created in the Divine image that strive to do good, and
therefore the obligation of the educator is to reveal the good in the
personality of the pupil, to encourage him to overcome his weak-
nesses.... The command is not heteronomous; it wells up from
within the person.[4]

## Conclusions and Application: Musar and the Religious Experience

All of this propels us to a certain conclusion about Musar. It must be
lived, not just learned. Progress in Musar is intertwined with the religious experience. In our time, the religious person needs to discover
and reinforce his capacity to distance himself from his instincts, to be
truly concerned with what is truly important. He needs to overcome
the lure of sophisticated superficiality posed by the environment (as
discussed in the preceding *shiur*). To do all this, we must look for
ways to open ourselves experientially. Traditional Musar literature
is in agreement with this, for it frequently criticizes externalized religious practice, and views as close to catastrophic what the prophet
describes – 'They have honored Me with their mouth and lips, but
their heart is far from Me, and their fear of Me has become as the
people's customary obligation' (Yeshayahu 29:13).

I know that I risk being misunderstood when I recommend the
religious experience as a way of awakening our higher inclinations.
We live in an age when the religious experience has been, to a great
extent, hijacked. It has come to be associated with people in search
of a 'high', and who value religion to the extent that it gives them the
states of bliss and higher consciousness they are seeking. But this is
not the experiential element that I have in mind. This view is as essentially egotistic as any other lifestyle typical of our times (though
more refined), and has nothing to do with the covenantal values (to

return to our familiar categories) that modern man finds hard to grasp. I am referring, rather, to the experience of the absolute moral claim that God makes on our lives, His demand that we surrender ourselves completely – and soulfully – to the tasks with which He charges us, the realization that there is a voice within us that echoes this demand and knows how true and just it is. Joy is certainly important in our world-view, but primarily as a commandment, a moral imperative – not merely an egotistical goal.

We are understandably awed by Rav Soloveitchik's stark description:

> The religious act is primarily an experience of suffering. When a person meets God, he is summoned to self-sacrifice, which is expressed in the struggle with primitive passions, breaking of the will, acceptance of a transcendental burden, forgoing excessive worldly pleasures, intermittent withdrawal from the sweet and pleasant and surrender to the bitter and the strange.... Bring your sacrifice! That is the main command given to the man of religion.[5]

But being awed is not the same as being 'turned off'. Our ability to realize that this is a suffering which purifies and enriches, a suffering which we need, is a mark of our maturity.

Are there ways of doing this? Are there methods that encourage the growth we desire? From here we turn to practice. Knowing the centrality of learning in Judaism, we will not be surprised to see that study, as in 'learning Musar,' is an important element in our quest. On the other hand, we will have to find ways of overcoming the insulation that separates mind from soul. *Be-ezrat Hashem*, this will be the next leg of our journey.

## Notes
1. The following example is based on the article by Feuerstein and Feuerstein quoted in the preceding lesson.
2. Rav Elisha Aviner, in *Idealism and Self-Realization*, ed. Ze'ev Karov (El-Ami, 5759/1999), pp. 21–22.
3. Rav Eliezer Scheinwald, 'Education Toward Self-Realization or *Komemiyut*', ibid., p. 27.

4. *Likutei Shoshanim: Anthology in Memory of Shoshana Lasker (Hebrew)*, ed. Dr. Yossi Green, 5760 (2000), p. 20.

5. 'On Love of Torah and Redeeming the Soul of the Generation,' in *Be-Sod Ha-Yachid Ve-Hayachad*, ed. Pinchas Peli (Jerusalem: Orot, 5736), p. 427.

# Shiur eleven

# Rav Yisrael Salanter's Technique

## PART I

W E WILL NOW begin to survey some of the practical techniques of Musar that have come down to us from the teachers of previous generations. As we shall see, all of these guidelines address the problem of turning intellectual effort into something that will have experiential impact on the inner reaches of our personalities.

The first approach, which we hope to examine in more than one version, was defined and popularized by Rav Yisrael Salanter, the founder of the modern (nineteenth-century) Musar movement. We will cite the description of Rav Shlomo Wolbe, a contemporary exponent of this approach.[1] Rav Wolbe calls this technique *hitbonenut*, which is usually translated as 'contemplation' or 'attention,' but as will become clear, the emphasis here is not necessarily intellectual.

> *Hitbonenut* is one of the great secrets of the Torah. This is how it was explicated by Ramchal (Rav Moshe Chayim Luzzatto) in his *Derekh Etz Chayim*:
>
> > 'See now that both of them – the human mind, and the Torah which informs it – are of the same character. 'Torah is light' – actual light, not mere wisdom. The Torah is compared to fire, for all its words and letters are like coals, in that when left alone they may appear to be only coals that are somewhat dim, but when one begins to

learn them they ignite. This is what characterizes the human mind as well, for its power of great understanding causes it to glow with the force of *hitbonenut*.'

This explains what is found in the introduction to *Mesilat Yesharim*, that 'the better-known these things are and the more the truths [of Musar] are obvious to all, so do we find them being ignored and forgotten.' The reason for this is that, since these facts are so widely known, *hitbonenut* regarding them is lacking, and therefore they lack the character of light, and are only wisdom, which means that their influence is hardly felt, and they are largely forgotten!

This, then, is the work of Musar.... We may know about Providence, but this knowledge has no light. We may know what our duty is in this world, but this knowledge has no light. *Hitbonenut* turns knowledge into light.

This is an instructive formulation of the difference between grasping knowledge and experiencing it. As Rav Wolbe continues to explain, the distinction is reflected practically in the two stages of the Musar 'session':

*Hitbonenut* has two stages. First, we delve into the text we are studying or into a particular saying of Chazal, in order to understand the structure of the topic, as in studying Gemara. In this stage, we should be careful not to treat the words as mere figures of speech that are not to be taken literally.... For example, when we learn in *Mesilat Yesharim* (chap. 2): 'The attribute of carefulness means that one should watch and attend to one's deeds and habits, whether they are good or not, so that one should not leave oneself open to the risk of ruin, God forbid,' the student should clarify the difference between 'deeds' and 'habits'. Likewise, 'risk of ruin' is not a figure of speech or an exaggeration, and one should clarify to oneself exactly what this ruin is....

In the second stage, the student should compare what he has learned from the text with his own situation, trying to define the extent of the disparity between the two, and its causes.

In this stage, our teacher, Rav Yisrael Salanter ל"ז, introduced his major innovation. He required immediate review of the saying (from the text) several times, but not a mere ordinary review, but 'with feeling of the soul, stormy spirit, and fiery lips.' In other words, this review must be done aloud and with melody, in order to arouse emotion and enthusiasm.

This type of review causes the subject to become even clearer; the heart burns with the realization of the disgrace of sin ...and the intense desire to purify and correct oneself. This enthusiasm leaves an impression in the heart even if one forgets it after a while. When Musar is learned daily, these subtle, invisible impressions become constantly stronger, and imprint one's entire behavior, without the person realizing it.

The division between objective analysis and creating existential attachment is clear. The analysis alone leaves us in the realm of theoretical wisdom. Once we identify theoretically with the ethical goal targeted by the text, the next stage aims to have it shape and strengthen our will. Hence, we have here an attempt to face ourselves on more existential levels – first by assessing our own status and position vis-à-vis the source being studied, and then making the source 'work' on us.

For our purposes, I would add a certain ingredient to this description. In our opening *shiurim* (particularly *shiur* 3), we discussed the problem of fitting the text to the reader. We noted that the student must be able to identify with the text in order to motivate himself to adopt its teaching in a practical way. Given this necessity, I think that this matter also should be addressed as part of the process. Recall that at the beginning of Rav Wolbe's second stage, I examine my situation in the light of the text and its message, noting the disparity. What is this disparity? Rav Wolbe means: the extent to which I do not adequately fulfill the teaching of the text. But we may add the necessity of checking for another potential disparity – the extent to which I fail to *identify* with the text. Is this source a challenge that is 'for me,' at this point in my life, in my present frame of mind (and so on with any other relevant variables)? It is advisable to hold open the possibility that my available time and effort may be better utilized with a different text. But if the message at hand does strike a sufficiently responsive chord within me, I decide to deepen my involvement with it.

However, the major innovation here is Rav Yisrael Salanter's teaching that reviewing the material while consciously trying to mobilize the forces of the will – earnestness, emotion, enthusiasm – is a technique that works. I can readily imagine that the novice may find this theory hard to accept. Rav Wolbe actually follows up the above outline with assurances that experience shows the value of this approach. He quotes the last testament of Rav Naftali Amsterdam, one of the three major disciples of Rav Yisrael Salanter:

> In general, I say to you that the thing that put me on my feet in matters of *avodat Hashem* was my learning of Musar in the manner that I learned from my teacher and master of blessed memory. On a day that I learn Musar, all my deeds, speech, and thoughts are better. The routine should be the following, as I heard from my teacher.... If, for example, one sets aside an hour for this study, then he should divide it in two: half an hour for studying the Musar text, as one would study any other material ...and the second half-hour to study with excitement, to learn a saying and repeat it many times.... This is how he himself used to learn.[2]

### What's in a 'technique'?

Now that we have had our first glimpse of a Musar technique, I would like to take 'time-out' for an important background discussion. We are looking for techniques to help us in our quest, and the question we will always ask ourselves is how well do they work, and which ones work the best. I would like now to delve a bit into the significance of the very concept of 'technique' in the realm of Musar. As we will see, this is not a matter of mere practical significance, but is laden with profound implications. One of the great contributions of Rav Yisrael Salanter was precisely his insistence, beyond the *definition* of the method, that there *are* methods. Why the emphasis on this point?

To illustrate, let us focus on the religious world of Lithuania in which Rav Yisrael made his appearance as a leader and educator, and what the impact of his approach was in that milieu.

The Lithuanian community was Halakha-oriented. When a person whose spiritual compass is Halakhic asks himself: "What does God want and expect of us?", his answer is: *behavior*, for that is the apparent concern of Halakha. Now we may ask this person, "What about the realm of emotion and belief, which is included in such *mitzvot* as fear of God, loving others, not bearing a grudge and so forth?" Our law-oriented Jew would likely tell us, that all that is also behavior. There is behavior of the body, and there is also behavior of the heart and mind. There is no real difference.

But we may further query the Halakhic mind-set: what happens when a person tries to refrain from undesirable or forbidden thoughts and feelings, and he finds controlling these exceedingly difficult? How does the Halakhic approach come to his aid? Our respondent will again reply, "There is nothing unusual here. What would you do if your *sukkah* fell down? You would put it up again, and make it stronger, drive in more nails, etc. I advise you to overcome your emotional problems the same way. Try again; *try harder.*"

This "quantitative" approach is the only one which presents itself, as long as we are oblivious to the concept of techniques. Rav Chaim of Volozhin, for instance, prescribed setting aside a certain amount of time for cultivating *yirat shamayim*. When addressing those who find the allotted time insufficient, his advice is that they devote more time. The Gaon of Vilna frequently uses the term *shevirat ha-midot* to describe personal moral elevation. The phrase implies that unwanted *midot* are meant to be 'broken'; it's all a matter of how hard, and how many times, you 'hit'. If the evil inclination is still with you, perhaps your hammer isn't heavy enough. Try a two-pounder instead of a one-pounder.[3]

At this point, the founder of the Musar movement appears with a pointed message. If the wall doesn't budge despite my earnest head-blows, the problem won't necessarily be solved by continuing the process with increased vigor. The reason I find it difficult to think and act as I should, is that there is a dissonance between myself and the *mitzva*. The approach must therefore be to try and apprehend the workings of the soul, and devise a thought-out, corrective strategy. What this means is that practically speaking, doing God's will is not only a matter of *behaving*, but also *being* and *becoming*.

The conclusion to be drawn is an identity, almost an equation if you will, which to my mind is momentous. To fulfill the Torah means to grow as a person, and to grow truly as a person is tantamount to the fulfillment of Torah. Given the mind-set of the Lithuanian community, we can well imagine that this novel idea would be perceived as vastly unsettling, an upheaval in religion comparable to Einstein's transfomation of the world of physics. Perhaps this is one of the roots of the opposition, some of it rather extreme, which Rav Yisrael encountered.

One final point, before getting back to the particular method under discussion. In order to talk about techniques, it was necessary for Rav Yisrael Salanter to make another subtle but profound modification – one that had to do with how we talk about the human personality. The reigning conception in traditional Eastern Europe was to view the soul of man as something mysterious, holy, and part of the Divine. This understanding was no doubt heavily based on the Kabbalah, but in fact it figures prominently in the Midrash as well. For example, the ancient Rabbis with their characteristic forthrightness, actually drew parallels between the human soul and God Himself:

> Just as the Holy One fills the world, so the soul fills the body. Just as the Holy One sees but is not seen, so the soul sees but is not seen…. Just as the Holy One is pure, so is the soul pure. Just as the Holy One dwells in the innermost chamber, so the soul dwells in the innermost chamber.[4]

Here is the traditional soul – untouchable and ineffable, invisible and mysterious. Such a soul poses a problem for the technique-oriented approach. For how can one presume to make changes in this exalted, transcendent essence? In fact, without saying it in so many words, Rav Yisrael changed the terms of discussion when discussing the personality. Of course we believe in the transcendent soul. But if we want to make soul-changes, Rav Yisrael knew that rather than talk about the soul itself, we ought to refer to what we know as the *mind*. The human mind is something that can be known, observed, analyzed and characterized. In his writings, Rav Yisrael actually used concepts which were current in the psychology of his time. He exploited these findings in order to devise and elucidate his guidance.

This last realization has ramifications for us. Assuming that psychological research has progressed since the days of the Musar movement, it may be worthwhile to explore more recent findings for a deeper and more precise appreciation of what 'makes us tick'. The renewed insight could shed light on the practical approaches to be found in the sources, and also generate beneficial new ones.

I hope this general discussion of techniques has been helpful. Let us get back to specifics. Previously we examined a classical formulation of Rav Yisrael Salanter's approach, the crux of which is the assimilation of conclusions arrived at intellectually into the total personality, thus influencing conduct. This direction was taken further by Rav Yosef Horowitz, the founder of the Novhardok school of Musar, who propagated this type of study in a distinctive, radical, fashion.

## The Novhardok Approach

We have already quoted Rav Horowitz's book, *Madregat Ha-Adam*. He analyzed the topic we are discussing under the heading 'Fear and Love' (chap. 14). Rav Horowitz argues that intellectual study is ill-suited to moral development. A word about Rav Horowitz's nomenclature in this matter: Intellectual study is designated 'mental effort', and it is contrasted with 'sensory effort', which corresponds to emotional, enthusiastic study. For Rav Horowitz, the 'mental-sensory' distinction is equivalent to 'abstract-actual'. He claims that sensory effort alone has the power to bring about actual change. Let us first see his description of mental effort:

Mental effort is when a person toils with his mind to understand the way of God, by learning Musar – but with the mind, not with enthusiasm…. His return is commensurate with his effort. Since he tries [for example] to understand the foundations upon which man can put his trust in God, and has delved into these matters with his mind, he is aware that everything that happens is dependent on God…. He has [also] arrived at the knowledge of what is truly good and what is truly bad….

But if he knows all this only with his mind and not with his senses, he will find that his mental effort yields only a mental [i.e., abstract] result, not a sensory [i.e., actual] one. As Chazal said, 'The wicked know that their fate is evil and bitter, but it is too hard for them to change.' Even though the mental effort enables him to quiet the ferment of human nature and evil attributes *while* he is speaking of moral ideals, he cannot at all master his predilections and forgo his passions and rejoice in the verdict of God [i.e., suffering]. This is so because his effort was not to educate himself to actually put things into practice, but only to mentally comprehend the proper world-view, the whole way of life, the 'how, what and when.'…

At the moment of trial, he is like a blind man who never saw the light, because then the cloud covers the sun and he can see nothing. All his exalted knowledge exists either before the fact or after the fact, but when the [trying] situation is at hand, the distraction of the trial makes him like a different man. In retrospect, he will say, 'At the time of the trial, I wasn't the same man that I am now, after the trial.'[5]

Rav Horowitz's frame of reference is somewhat different from the one we have used until now. His approach to Musar is oriented to 'trial' (*nisayon*). We have been talking about the need for change in the sense of moral growth. The Novhardoker would view this goal as an abstract mental category. The aim, according to him, is not to make one's 'deeds, speech and thoughts better,' as Rav Naftali Amsterdam put it. The problem is more pressing, because man is constantly beset with trying situations. Man's overriding mission is to respond to every trial the right way. If he tries to learn how to do this by expending only intellectual effort, the proposition is hopeless, because – para-doxically – the very character of mental study is totally different from its professed objective. The study is abstract and theoretical, but the situation poses a real life-challenge.

Therefore, the only solution is to marshal the existential forces of the soul. This is the meaning of the sensory, real-life effort. Rav Horowitz upgrades the importance of enthusiasm (*hitpaʾalut*) in Mu-sar. Unlike Rav Wolbe's more classical description, Rav Horowitz does not talk about an hour-long session divided into two equal halves. I imagine that he would concede the necessity of first intellectually comprehending the content, but the real effort, the major challenge, is *limud be-hitpaʾalut*.

What remains to be understood is how *hitpaʾalut* solves the prob-lem. How, according to Rav Horowitz, does this equip one to weather moral challenges successfully? This matter is clarified with the help of another distinction which he makes between mental and sensory effort. We will continue from this point in our next *shiur,* and thus gain a fuller understanding of the rationale of Rav Horowitz's method.

## Notes

1. *Alei Shur*, vol. 1, pp. 89–91.
2. For what it is worth, I would add that Zvi Kurzweil, in *Directions in Jewish Education* (Tel Aviv: Am Oved, 1981), points out a basic similarity between this technique and the spiritual exercises of non-Jewish mystics. While it is clear that Rav Yisrael was in no way influenced by anything other than Jewish sources, Kurzweil maintains that the common denominator shows that he hit upon a basic truth of the religious personality that was recognized by men of different persuasions. I have not examined this matter, but my fleeting impression is that the Musar methodology differs fundamentally from the non-Jewish examples in that its emphasis is moral, not mystical. Rav Yisrael Salanter actually opposed mysticism from an educational standpoint. But this requires closer inspection of the evidence. Kurzweil relies on Huxley's *The Perennial Philosophy*, James's *The Varieties of Religious Experience*, and Evelyn Underhill's *Mysticism*.
3. This discussion of mine is guilty of generalization. Techniques do appear in the works of the predecessors of Rav Yisrael Salanter, going back at least to the Rambam. But I am crediting Rav Yisrael with the renewal of the emphasis on this concept and the attempt to disseminate it on an unprecedented scale.

4. Berakhot 10b.
5. The style of *Madregat Ha-Adam* is unique, and difficult (for me!) to translate. I therefore found it necessary to take some liberties in the rendering. But I believe I am being faithful to the spirit of the original.

# Shiur twelve

# Rav Yisrael Salanter's Technique
## PART II

IN OUR LAST *shiurim*, we became acquainted with the two- stage format of learning Musar standardized by Rav Yisrael Salanter. We also began to see how this approach was developed by Rav Yosef Horowitz of Novhardok. He laid heavy emphasis on the second stage, designating it 'sensory effort,' and crediting it as the exclusive means of improving one's capacity to successfully meet *nisyonot* (trials). This is opposed to 'mental effort,' which may grant understanding, but not the practical capacity to put one's knowledge to use in difficult situations. We left off with the question of why *hitpaʾalut* (enthusiasm) is so much more effective in this regard than intellection.

Rav Horowitz gives us his answer by further exploring the contrast between mental and sensory learning (*Madregat Ha-Adam*, Fear and Love, chap. 15):

> The mind is an all-encompassing force, in which attention to one thing does not cause one to forget another. For example, when someone thinks about how great his spiritual deficiency is, he is simultaneously aware that his level is superior to that of his fellows. At the same time that he thinks that he must repent from his evil ways, he thinks about how people will mock and misunderstand him if he does. And when he thinks about how great the ways of

our forefathers were, he thinks that he will never achieve their level. The result is that he will never begin to do anything, not even a hairsbreadth of *teshuva* (repentance).

But the force of *hitpaʿalut*, on the other hand, is in its gathering all the different winds to a solitary point, and this point outweighs everything in the whole world, overruling all hindrances, barriers, and contrary considerations. Everything appears to him as naught with respect to the point of his *hitpaʿalut*, and all of his aims, wants, and ambitions unite to seek the actualization of that point. All his intolerance, anger, and cruelty unite to rage against the hindrances and considerations that come to prevent the achievement of the point of his *hitpaʿalut*, and all of his sensory, mental, and physical capacity unites to actualize the point of his *hitpaʿalut*....

Therefore *hitpaʿalut* is the sole vehicle of sensory effort. Without it, it is impossible to transform oneself, or to make unlimited demands of oneself.

We have tasted here something of the revolutionary atmosphere of Novhardok. The vocabulary reflects a powerful emotional arsenal – rage, cruelty, unlimited demands – meant to be mobilized in the cause of Torah ethics. This climate is not home to ordinary intellectual study.

If we were to define the aim of *hitpaʿalut* according to Rav Horowitz, the key word is *teviʿa* – 'demand.' This is a goal at which rational considerations cannot arrive. True, one could decide, on the strength of reason alone, to take a moral initiative. But the mind can easily summon counter-arguments to any proposition. The decision to act is always based on 'majority,' the pros having outweighed the cons. This makes any decision inherently tentative, for once action is begun, and once the environment becomes hostile, the difficulties that abound for those who would advance spirituality in our imperfect world suddenly make the array of considerations look different. The enormity of the task, the risk of shame and ridicule, now make cessation of action appear the most logical step. Yesterday's cowardice becomes today's discretion; what we thought was integrity is now perceived as hopelessly quixotic. No, rational decision is too weak a foundation for moral achievement. Only the *demand* will give us the willpower we need – the demand that comes from within. *Hitpaʿalut* is the vehicle of demand: 'when he learns in a tone of demand, with arguments of demand, his heart demanding that he complete his deficiency.'

The Rav of Novhardok goes on to polemicize against those who question the necessity and value of all this:

> This is why all the arguments against the enthusiastic learning of Musar – 'Why all the cries? Why the noise?' – collapse. To the contrary, the onus is on the questioner: Why is your spirit cold when it comes to the ruin of your soul in both worlds, but you get excited about your body and your wealth, which will only lead to aggravation and pain in this world, and disgrace and calumny in the next? You are the one who has reversed the correct priorities....
>
> *Hitpaʿalut* lifts the fog and chases away the clouds. A clear light, the light of wisdom, shines before us, and we see a new world, a different reality. This strengthens us more and more, until all our feelings unite to yearn only for that one point of truth.... There is no limit to what one can achieve by learning Musar. Anyone can reach the point where nothing is too difficult in his eyes for the sake of fulfilling the Torah.

Let us recap what we have seen so far. The classic approach of Rav Yisrael Salanter uses *hitpaʿalut* to break down the barrier between mind and soul. The specific concept of Musar that one has studied, grasped, and formulated is made to penetrate the personality with concentrated, earnest repetition and review. The school of Novhardok uses *hitpaʿalut* not in the context of a particular teaching of Musar, but more as a means of deepening and fortifying one's basic commitment. The idea is to create a mindset of total devotion to one point – the pursuit of *sheleimut* (wholeness), being almost obsessively concerned with its achievement, and fearlessly mocking, belittling, and ignoring all obstacles.

If this is the first time you have been exposed to the approach of Novhardok, it probably has not left you indifferent. I suggest that we now take a look at a different approach. This will give us a more complete picture of the variations possible in the context of Rav Yisrael Salanter's basic technique. Then each of us can decide which version, if any, we can use to help ourselves.

## The Technique According to *Shiurei Da'at*

In the following passage, another exponent of Rav Yisrael Salanter's technique, Rav Yosef Leib Bloch, rosh yeshiva of Telz, offers his advice on 'how to do it':

> A person should not force himself to learn with enthusiasm. He should not try to coerce his thoughts and energies towards this, because this way is unnatural. Furthermore, someone who 'pulls' the enthusiasm forcibly …will not succeed, because the other forces and emotions that reside within him will not let one of the forces loose to be aroused and exalted by itself; they will not leave it alone. At this time more than any other, the *yetzer* (impulse) that disturbs and hinders thought stands vigilantly on guard so as not to allow the exalted emotion in man to achieve the pure, inner arousal which this sacred study ought to bring.
>
> So it is. Man does not have the power to arouse his good feelings by forcing his nature; he cannot detach and hold the feeling of enthusiasm and excitement just in order to learn Musar; he cannot, at that time, push away all that lives within him, to drive the *yetzer* from his heart….
>
> But rather this is the way to learn Musar: The whole man, with all of his capacities and feelings, the man as he is, should learn Musar. He begins to learn calmly and patiently, with a sweet voice and profound observation; he hears every word he utters, examines it and feels it. The study, together with the pleasant and stimulating melody, energizes and brings the whole man to heartfelt inner enthusiasm…. Then the whole man becomes exalted – his whole essence, the man with everything in him.[1]

Rav Bloch is sensitive to the tug-of-war that goes on between the various voices within us. In this, he is no different from the Rav of

Novhardok. But the latter is sure that if we only abandon our commitment to intellectualism, we will possess the sense and sensitivity to be able to unite all of our turbulent emotions for the sake of 'one single point.' The author of *Shiurei Da'at*, however, considers the attempt to arrive at this result through conscious effort as virtually futile. This is a rather extreme contrast! Both of these men spoke from wide educational experience, and the spectacle of such diametrically opposing views conjures up the bewildering anomaly that is the dread of Talmudic scholars – the *machloket bi-metziut*, a disagreement over fact. How could there be such different opinions about the reality of human nature? Which of these wise men is the one with impaired eyesight? I believe that the only reasonable conclusion is that they both were describing a reality that they knew to be true about themselves and, by and large, their students. Their styles and philosophies were patently different, and each attracted the disciples about whom the generalizations they made would indeed be true. This brings us back to the necessity of evaluating ourselves with respect to the differing viewpoints.

But let us continue to examine Rav Bloch's position. Granted, one cannot take oneself by storm. What then? Rav Bloch holds that the emotional stance needed in Musar is not demand (the very idea of demand pits one part of the self against the other), but rather harmony, openness, melodious sweetness. The only reliable way to progress is to avoid inner conflict, and this means that the *whole* self must see what a good idea Musar is.

There is a further innovation in the way Rav Bloch builds the relationship between the technique's two stages. According to him, the only direct action that we take is the study itself. True, we study with anticipation in our hearts – we are hopefully expecting to be elevated. But Rav Yisrael Salanter's second stage – if and when it comes about – is more or less automatic. See how Rav Bloch describes the passage from study to emotion:

The bottom line is that Musar must be learned like any other subject, with patience and careful study, and then in a natural way one becomes inspired by its holy words, which are full of sayings that stimulate and elevate the human soul.

And, once the holy words have been taken to heart, and the heartstrings are aroused, we can no longer prescribe the method of study, but quite naturally one is stimulated and becomes more and more enthusiastic, and learns with a loud voice and an excited, outpouring soul.

There is a problem here. This technique forgoes the conscious effort to stimulate emotion, and hopes that it will happen. And what if it doesn't? Rav Bloch continues:

And even if, after all this, his soul is not aroused, and his heart does not fill up with sacred song, if after learning Musar this way he does not become enthusiastic – let it be. Even such Musar study is meaningful.

If I understand correctly, he means that the impression made on our soul is not always immediately apparent. Growth can occur in small increments that may be seen only in the long run.

## Summation and Closing Comments

Let us offer a brief characterization of the techniques we have studied in the last two *shiurim*. To start from the end, Novhardok and *Shiurei Da'at* differ fundamentally. The former is motivated by the need to successfully meet life's constant challenges; its psychological goal is to leap unhesitatingly, to fling oneself courageously into the higher life of Torah ideals. The latter approach distrusts this posture and finds it unstable. Natural, guided spiritual growth is to be preferred; study is important because it provides the wings of inspiration.

But despite the difference between them, they share a common focus. If we were to ask what lies beyond the intellectual study of Musar, what is the transcending goal that we wish to achieve, both Rav Horowitz and Rav Bloch would answer that their techniques directly influence one's most basic spiritual level, one's existential attachment to Torah. This, I believe, is not generally the case in Rav Yisrael's approach as we saw it in the previous *shiur*. There the goal was to 'turn knowledge into light,' to take a *particular* goal of Musar and make the knowledge of it effective, assimilate it, feel it profoundly.

As is usual in such matters, it is up to the individual to decide whether to apply any given approach. I would emphasize that it is not an either/or proposition. A person may at times find himself in need of a moral 'shaking-out,' and then may be helped by Rav Horowitz's assurance that this is something that can be done. At other times one's whole personality may be more in need of generosity, the ego suffering morally from neglect and in need of sublimation; this would call for a different method.

Before closing, one more comment about the Novhardok school. The practice of leveling demands on oneself borders on something else that we have already dealt with: severe self-reproach or browbeating. If this border is crossed, the whole technique is at serious risk. Making great demands of oneself can be done in earnest only in the context of positive, healthy self-appraisal. Sinking into the quagmire of self-reproach is anathema to progress, and I am sure that Rav Horowitz did not have this in mind. For confirmation of this, please refer to the citation from his *Madregat Ha-Adam* back in *shiur* 6. However, many people would probably fail to make this distinction, and for them, following the approach of Novhardok could be a perilous mistake.

We will end here our discussion of Rav Yisrael's method and its derivatives. In our next *shiur*, we will continue our survey of Musar techniques with a method that antedates the ones we have so far addressed.

### Notes
1. *Shi'urei Da'at*, vol. 2, p. 200.

# Shiur thirteen

# The Depth of Mind

OUR LAST two *shiurim* concentrated on the technique of Rav Yisrael Salanter and its variations. Nowadays, when most people speak of Musar, the term has a narrow connotation alluding to the nineteenth-century Musar movement. However, in this book we are using the word in the broader sense of the study of 'how to live'. In pursuing our survey of the practical means at our disposal in the task of spiritual and ethical progress, we will from here on follow in the wake of other schools of thought found in Jewish sources.

The methods of learning Musar that we have studied until now were generated by the dichotomy of mind and emotion. The assumption was that substantial change needs the vehicle of emotion in order to achieve depth. The path we will take now, however, is different. It takes mind alone as the exclusive point of departure and the prime focus of activity. Yet, as we shall see, the contribution of mind per se to ethical growth is not so easily understood. This is why the sources we will examine tend to cross over to the super-rational.

We will introduce this viewpoint with Rav Elimelekh Bar-Shaul, the late rabbi of Rechovot, from his collection of essays called *Ma'arkhei Lev* (p. 11):

> 'Many are the thoughts in the heart of a man' – Great, rich thoughts, and small, poor ones. Thoughts that rise to the very crucible of existence, and thoughts that address ordinary daily life. Thoughts

as calm as placid waters, and thoughts that storm like turbulent waves. Stable, continuous thoughts, and thoughts of revolution and breakthrough. Ripe, clear thoughts, and premature, obfuscated thoughts.

Rav Bar-Shaul is telling us that the mind is not merely a vessel that absorbs knowledge, an instrument that analyzes facts or orchestrates reactions to external stimuli. Our mind is better described as a fountainhead of thought. The ideas it produces are not monotonous, bland statements. They have color and character. They are distinguished from one another not only by content, but also by form and texture.

From here we proceed to the distinction that will be the theme of Rav Bar-Shaul's discussion. The coming ideas are abstract, but be patient – the practical ramifications are waiting in the wings!

> There are inner thoughts and external thoughts. The inner thoughts are the ones that have not been 'carved' into letters, that have yet to come down to the level of explication. 'Thoughts precede all letters. They constantly roam about in our inwardness. We have to discover our true courage …in order to always be aware of the nature of those unimagined imaginings, those forms that are beyond all form, in order that we should recognize the glory of our soul' (- from Rav Kook's *Rosh Milin* 1).
>
> The inner thoughts are the ones that are projected directly from the recesses of the soul. We look inward and sense that 'the life-activity of the soul never ceases, just as physical life-activity never ceases throughout life. The manifestation of the mental life, which comes about because some bright new ideas are thought of from time to time – it seeming to us that time elapses between one new thought and the next – does not come from the basic, essential capacity of life, but from its outbranching manifestations. But the essence of life, which is the activity of the soul in its depths, never ceases at all. The thoughts constantly are created and stream inside us' (ibid. 137)….
>
> The primal depth of human thought, the source from which

light flows to the inner thought and from there to all thoughts, is invisible to us. Yet that is the essence of thought and the essence of man, as opposed to all the other thoughts and ruminations that pass through the human mind, which are not the main part of thought, but only the garb of the inner thought....

The bottom line of all this for us, on our level of understanding, is this: thought is superficial and external, if it does not plumb the depths to the source of thought.... Only when thought has deepened to the source of its sustenance will it be illuminated from within.

However, deepening of this sort is possible only through study of Torah.

We will pause here to catch our breath. This account of the activity of the mind is new for us, and it contrasts sharply with the conception of the intellect as a tool for interacting with the environment (compare with the citation from Georg Simmel in lesson 9). Such interaction is treated here as the most external, nonessential function of mind. But the essential mind is nontransparent, virtually ineffable. The thoughts that become intelligible to us are derivatives, or 'garments,' of the inner intellect. From this description of the reality, we arrive at a presumptuous program; we can use our revealed intelligence to establish contact with the world of inner thought, which is beyond clear conception. Our defined thinking can plumb the depths of the mysterious mind, and thus become 'illuminated from within.' The vehicle for this communication is Torah.

You no doubt sense the mystical aura that surrounds all this. This strain becomes more pronounced in the following quotations. To support his claim, Rav Bar-Shaul cites the *Derekh Etz Ha-Chayim of Ramchal* (Rav Moshe Chayim Luzzatto):

The Torah is not like other branches of knowledge and secular sciences.... Torah is sacred, and possesses a reality that is celestial. When someone learns Torah in the lower world, it is a light that illuminates his soul and connects it to the upper secret chambers of the Holy One, by way of the illumination and the powerful influence it exerts upon it.[1]

He also cites this kabbalistic doctrine, from Rav Chayim of Volozhin (*Nefesh Ha-Chayim* 1:16):

> Chazal have told us in no uncertain terms that the only way to
> achieve the sparks of the soul's light is through intensive study of
> our holy Torah, for both of these derive from the same source, as
> is known to the wise.

The mystical theory here is important to the author as a basis for
his conclusions, but he is not recommending 'transcendental' practices. He is, rather, following Rav Chayim Volozhiner in claiming that
intensive study of *revealed* Torah leads to the discovery of thoughts
that are of profound *inner* significance. Torah is a light in the soul
because it is the soul's cognate, issuing from the same supernatural
Divine source. Thoughts of Torah belong to the world of thoughts of
the innermost soul.

Rav Bar-Shaul believes that this is especially true of that part of
Torah that deals most directly with Musar and *midot* (character traits).
He quotes Rabbenu Yona's *Sha'arei Teshuva* (3:15):

> Of those who do not devote thought to the study of the fear of God,
> it says: 'And their fear of Me is merely as a people's customary ob-
> ligation,' and also, 'You are close in their mouths but far from their
> reins.' ...But of those who think, study intensively, and draw near
> [to God], it says, 'And I am always with you, You have held My right
> hand ...and as for me, the proximity to God is good for me.'

To put it succinctly, the directive here is for in- depth study of
Torah, particularly Musar. Depth of study reveals the person's own
personal understanding and original insights in this area, and these
are a unique revelation of his inner self. Such study, ostensibly intellectual, develops and builds the personality. Rav Bar-Shaul concludes:

> No one can know himself unless he has discovered the light of his
> soul. And this light is revealed only if he has achieved the light of
> Torah. The effort of Torah study and in-depth Torah thinking are
> great illuminations of the soul ...the heart, and the whole being. It

is all one light – the light of Torah, which is the light of the soul, which is the light of thought, which is the light of man.

I would like to draw attention to the contrast between this and what we learned in our very first *shiur* in the name of the Vilna Gaon. The Gaon wrote that Torah study is often not a moral influence, and can even have a negative effect on the personality. Is there a conflict here? Not necessarily. Rav Bar-Shaul is talking to a person who is interested in growth and ethical progress. For one with such a positive orientation, profound Torah study holds out the promise of help in actualizing his potential. The Gaon, on the other hand, was warning us that if the 'seed' within the man is evil, Torah can conceivably make matters worse by exacerbating his already-present negative tendencies.

Admittedly, the theory here presented is one that may leave the rational-minded among us hanging, with a feeling of less-than-full understanding. At the same time, regardless of our level of comprehension, the example of genuine Torah scholars whose ethical stature was clearly and positively shaped by their years of intensive study speaks loudly.

## Meditation in Chasidut

Let us go a step further. The attempt to connect with the depth of thought within us may take a more direct turn in the form of meditation. While this practice is commonly connected with mysticism, it can be used to assimilate and deeply identify with principles of Musar, with the aim of making them a source of profound influence in our lives.

Meditation of this sort is discussed in the literature of Chabad (Lubavitch). The instructions that follow, based on Chabad sources, are from a book called *Betach Ba-Hashem*, by Rav David Rosen. The subject of the book is the attribute of *bitachon* (trust in God).[2] In chapter 8, meditation (rendered here as *hitbonenut*) is discussed as one of the means of changing one's *midot* in general.

> Meditation is done in two stages: in the first, one must expend effort
> to study the subject expansively ...to bring things down from their

abstraction and to illustrate and imagine them as far as possible, until he feels that he has gotten the message of the matter …and he is able to summarize the idea and the subject in one or two sentences….

But in order to arrive at understanding of the heart, one must continue to the next stage, in which one uses the power of *da'at* (literally, knowledge). *Da'at* means attachment and connection, as in 'And Adam knew (*yada*) Chava.' In other words, after precise study, the student must attach and connect himself to the object of study, in order that it become part of himself, so that he should not have the feeling that he and the subject learned are two things, that his study is foreign to him. On the contrary, he should reach the state in which he feels connection, identification, belonging, and unity with what he has learned.

We will presently return to this passage. But first note that the intellectual category *da'at* is given the force of the added connotation 'connection.' This idea is found in the foundational work of Chabad, the *Tanya* (chap. 3):

*Da'at* is [meant] as in [the verse,] 'And Adam knew Chava,' connoting connection and attachment, meaning that he [i.e., the meditator] attaches his *da'at* with a very strong, powerful connection, and tightly fastens his thought to the greatness of Ein Sof [the Infinite], blessed be He. Now if he does not attach his *da'at* and fasten his thought tightly and continuously, he will not succeed in producing within himself genuine love and fear.

In Chabad, the mind is the archetypal vehicle of connection, because the object of knowledge – a fact or a concept – is grasped and 'surrounded' by it. The connection is at once abstract and real. If the thought is strong and tight, the connection becomes even more apparent and actual. Of course, the author of the *Tanya*, Rav Shneur Zalman, is talking about meditation on the greatness of Ein Sof, a patently mystical meditation, though it certainly has ethical ramifications. Our purpose in bringing this technique is to utilize it in the more explicitly ethical sphere – meditation on a concept or teaching of Musar. Getting back to *Betach Ba-Hashem*:

> So it is specifically regarding the rectification of a moral attribute that the person and the idea studied must unite…. In this thought process one must pay attention to two things (without which there can be no connection or attachment). The first is *concentration*; that is, the person exerts himself to the utmost of his ability to tie his thought and hold it on the subject upon which he meditates, without losing attention. This is very important, because if the person does not tie his mind tightly and continuously without distraction from the object of his meditation, he will not achieve understanding of the heart. For loss of attention greatly weakens thought and handicaps its potential influence on the heart, and the result is that the moral attribute in question will remain unrectified.
>
> The second thing that requires attention is *duration*. The meditator must hold each thought for a certain amount of time, because a fleeting thought, which does not persist in the mind, does not have the power to penetrate the heart and work upon it. Just like in sin (as Chazal say), 'The eye sees, the heart desires, and the body's agents of action carry out the deed,' a parallel process characterizes spiritual progress. The 'eye sees' – proper meditation influences the heart, and then the heart desires, and the agents of action complete the rectification of the moral attribute in question.

I will not go beyond this basic description of the meditation process. Those interested can learn more from the extensive literature on the topic (the writings of Rav Aryeh Kaplan deserve mention), and also in courses and workshops given for people who want to develop the skill.

It is important to emphasize that our recommendation of this practice, as an avenue of spiritual improvement for those so inclined, applies exclusively to meditation done and taught in the spirit of Chasidut and Torah Judaism. Training and guidance given by teachers who represent thought-systems outside of Judaism can be hazardous, and frequently involve serious halakhic problems. A further word of caution is in order: one who seeks to develop the skill beyond the very basic level we have described should do so only with the guidance of an experienced teacher. The more advanced levels are, of course, relevant mainly to mystically oriented meditation, and less important for the purposes that interest us here.

It is time to retrace our steps and get a perspective on our survey thus far. Heretofore, we viewed the mind mainly as a prologue, with emotion as the vehicle of existential identification with the ethical ideal. In this *shiur* we have seen that the mind itself can be used not only as a means of understanding, but also as a way of achieving assimilation and identification. This can be done through intensive, creative study in depth. Meditation as taught by Chasidut – a process that grants power and continuity to thought – is another way of achieving unity. In trying to understand both the theory and practice of these approaches, we found ourselves crossing the dividing-line between rationalism and mysticism.

We began our survey of techniques by suggesting a balance between intellect and emotion; we continued with an approach that de-emphasizes emotion and relies heavily upon thought. Our next step will conserve the overall symmetry; it will feature an approach that has an opposite emphasis. This is a tradition that distrusts the mind, and sees emotion as the premier, reliable vehicle of ethical ascent. Such is the teaching of Rav Nachman of Braslav.

### Notes

1. This idea was also quoted from Ramchal by Rav Wolbe (above, shiur 11), but he proceeded from here to the assumption that intellectual study is not sufficient to get to the 'light'. Rav Bar-Shaul, like Rav Chayim Volozhiner, infers that the study itself is a way of linking up with the light of Torah and the soul.
2. The book is recommended, by the way, as a good, thorough treatment of the subject, based on primary sources.

## Shiur fourteen

# Ethical Ascent Through Prayer

## PART I

THE OBJECT of our inquiry is how to make good the apparent shortfall that intellectual study leaves – the gap between knowing and being. Rav Nachman of Braslav takes a unique position in our field of study. He believed that little is to be expected from our efforts to change ourselves through rational human effort. Actual progress is made exclusively on the basis of an activity that is an exercise of will and emotion; namely, prayer.

The source in Chazal that furnishes the basis for Rav Nachman's approach is the following *gemara* (Avoda Zara 5b):

> The Rabbis taught [on the verse] 'Who would grant that this heart of theirs be with them, to fear Me and keep all My commandments all the days?' (Devarim 5:26). Moshe said to Israel: Ungrateful sons of ungrateful fathers! When the Holy One said to Israel, 'Who would grant that this heart of theirs be with them,' they ought to have said, 'You grant it.'

This *gemara* is cited in the introduction to *Hishtapkhut Ha-Nefesh* ('The Outpouring of the Soul,' an anthology of Rav Nachman's sayings relevant to our topic),[1] and is followed there by the comment of Maharsha:

Even though Chazal said, 'Everything is in the hands of Heaven except the fear of Heaven,' it is nevertheless obvious that the Holy One can tilt the heart of men for the better, for many verses prove this.

Rav Nachman went on from this interesting midrash to propagate the practice of what he called *hitbodedut* (loosely translated as 'aloneness' or 'seclusion'). We immediately notice the similarity in sound between this and *hibonenut*, but the difference is crucial. *Hitbodedut* is devoid of any intellectual connotation. The meaning of the word has to do with the isolation of the prayer setting, as well as the uniqueness and personal nature of the prayer itself (as in 'a nation that dwells *badad* [alone]' – Bamidbar 23:9). As *Hishtapkhut Ha-Nefesh* continues:

From all this it is clear to the eye to what extent Chazal encouraged *hitbodedut*, that is, expression in speech before God, blessed be He, and beseeching Him to give us fear of Heaven so that we do not sin. Even though 'all is in the hands of Heaven except for fear of Heaven,' nonetheless everything is in His hand. One must pray to God Himself for this, as it says explicitly in this *gemara*, that Moshe criticized them severely and called them ungrateful because they did not say to God, 'You give us,' that is, that God give them fear of Heaven.

Rav Nachman, then, requires us to ask for Divine intervention to make us better. He is aware that this conflicts with the saying of Chazal that the fear of Heaven is not in the hands of Heaven. This aphorism is a popular rendition of the principle of free will and choice, which is one of the touchstones of the traditional Jewish outlook, and without which reward and punishment would be impossible. Rav Nachman maintains that 'nonetheless everything is in His hand,' including fear of Heaven.

Exactly how this squares with the above saying of Chazal is something that remains to be seen. But we should at the same time concede the truth of the Maharsha's statement, namely, that there is evidence in Scripture for the thesis that God's intervention in the state of human ethics is indeed possible. We use many of these Scriptural references in our standard *Selichot* prayers, when we ask God, for example, to 'circumcise our hearts so that we may love His name.' God's hardening of Pharaoh's heart is a famous example of human depravity imputed by the Torah to Divine influence (this case, in fact, troubled the Rambam and other *Rishonim*). Another instance, from Yechezkel (36:27): 'And I will put My spirit within you, and I will make it so that you will walk in My statutes.' There are several ways of explaining these verses so that they do not pose an assault on free choice, but Rav Nachman cannot be accused of deviating from their spirit by taking them literally.

To gain perspective on this point, it is worthwhile to consider the opinion of the Gaon of Vilna, as stated in *Kol Eliyahu* (Sukka 52b). He too realizes the necessity of Divine help in overcoming the evil inclination. However, he does not draw the conclusion that man's main effort should be directed toward appealing for assistance from above. Quite the opposite – man must exercise his autonomy to the greatest extent possible, and only then can he expect help.

> Even though the Creator has given man the power to subdue his inclination by means of the spirit within him, the task cannot be completed by man, for it is very difficult for man to finish it. It is within his power only to begin the task and do whatever he can, whereas the completion of the work is through Divine assistance.... Now God is the judge of what is within man's heart, and He knows at what point a person has done whatever he can. And when He sees that someone has done what was in his power, and can do no more though he strongly desires only good, then does Divine assistance accompany him from on high. ...For he has come to the absolute limit of what he can do with his own action, and it is impossible for him to do more.... But if he still can do more than what he has done and he does not do it, God will not help him either.

Why does the Braslaver shun rational efforts to raise one's spiritual level? And how does he handle Chazal's insistence on free choice? Both of these questions are addressed in the following passage. The theory is kabbalistic, but we will see what can be deduced from it in simpler terms. (All of our citations from Rav Nachman will be from

*Hishtapkhut Ha-Nefesh*, by paragraph number. What follows is from paragraph 93.)

At first glance, one can raise a difficulty regarding the practice of *hitbodedut* and conversation with one's Maker …and also regarding the fact that all the righteous ones of old did this and composed numerous prayers in order to merit being saved from the *yezter ha-ra* and coming close to God…. Now Chazal said that 'Everything is in the hands of Heaven except the fear of Heaven.' If so, how is it possible to pray for this, since God has given the choice over to us exclusively? But the truth is that this is itself is man's main choice. For it is impossible for one to achieve wholeness and loathe evil and choose good and attain what one is supposed to attain in this world simply by using one's choice. Rather must one multiply prayers and entreaties …so that the multitude of evil waters – the evil desires of this world that are constantly raging – should not wash him away…. For even though man has free choice, the main thing is to pray and beseech God about this. For choice – the power to choose good and despise evil – is in the mind. But the human mind only has the power to subdue the lusts and *kelipot* [spiritual sources of defilement] that come from the aspect of heresy that results from the 'breaking of the vessels,' which hold sparks of holiness that are sparks of *intelligence*…. But there are confusions and 'other sides' [euphemism for the *yetzer ha-ra*] and obstacles to holiness that come from the aspect of 'the empty space,' where His Divinity cannot be found through any intelligence or wisdom, *but only by faith alone.* And this is the aspect of prayer, entreaties, and cries to God to save us from the *kelipot* and the *yetzer ha-ra* that come from there…. For in no way can one be saved from the *yetzer ha-ra* that comes from the 'empty space' with free choice and mind alone, but only with Divine assistance …Because intelligence there is of no avail. On the contrary, there intelligence and wisdom can cause one to sink even more, God forbid.

Rav Nachman (like the Rav of Novhardok, you will recall), develops a theory to explain the limitations of mind. Why don't we behave the way we know we ought to? Why, at times, does our mind even lead us astray? His answer is that, metaphysically speaking, evil comes in two formats. One of them is the 'broken vessels' that hold sparks of intelligence in captivity. These are situations in which the mind is imprisoned; but then there is also the theoretical possibility of setting it free. Clear, objective thinking liberates the person from the hold of the broken vessels. This struggle can be won with free choice, and this is the realm wherein Chazal said that 'it is up to man.'

But Rav Nachman thinks that this source of evil is not the main problem. There are moral defects in the world that do stem, not from lack of proper thinking, but from lack of faith. All of those great thinkers who arrived at conclusions with negative, even disastrous, moral repercussions, were not at all guilty of faulty argumentation. They merely demonstrated that in the empty space – the realm where evil comes about because of the lack (so to speak) of Divinity – intelligence can make matters worse by weakening faith. Rav Nachman here makes a daring statement about the fundamental inability of intelligence to find truth (as opposed to the approach of Novhardok, which saw mind as an appropriate instrument for dealing with trying situations).

This passage also illuminates the nature of the prayer effort that is Rav Nachman's main prescription. He is not saying that since man is incapable of helping himself by using his intelligence, he must therefore take a basically passive stance, awaiting the mercy of God, shrugging off responsibility with the assertion that 'I believe' (an idea found in the non-Jewish world). Faith is, rather, a weapon to be used against the confusion generated by the evil of the 'empty space'. The prayer effort is an expression and a deepening of faith, and Rav Nachman requires this effort to be an ongoing one. The resulting spiritual ascent, when it comes, is the answer to a prayer. Therefore it is the result of free Divine intervention, but on the other hand, of human striving as well.

## Making a Prayer Out of Torah

The Braslaver's lack of confidence in intellectual study led him to devise a formula that gives knowledge an existential turn (par. 2):

> Also, it is good to make a prayer out of the Torah. That is, when one learns or hears a sermon of Torah from a true *tzaddik*, then he should make a prayer out of it. In other words: to ask and beseech God for all [the spiritual levels] that are discussed in that sermon; when will he merit that he too should attain all of this, and how far removed he is from this. And he should ask God to grant that he attain whatever is discussed in that sermon.

The term 'Torah' here refers to an ethical or spiritual teaching of a *tzaddik*, or Chasidic master (primarily Rav Nachman himself). Intellectual knowledge of the teaching is virtually trivial; the daunting task is to carry it out, to actually achieve the coveted spiritual level described in the 'Torah.' Rather than struggle to apply the teaching in daily life, the main effort should be invested in turning to God for specific help in reaching the desired goal.

## *Hitbodedut:* Unique and Solitary

Rav Nachman is talking about spontaneous prayer. He frequently uses the term *sicha*, which Chazal sometimes used in the context of prayer, but which more frequently means 'speech' or 'conversation.'

> This prayer and this speech should be in the spoken language, that is, Yiddish (in our country). Because in the holy tongue [Hebrew] it will be difficult for him to express whatever he wants to say, and also the heart will not flow after the words because he is not used to the language …But in Yiddish he can express whatever he wants to say, and can say whatever is in his heart and talk about it before Him, blessed be He – whether it be regret and penitence about the past, or entreaties to merit actual nearness to Him from this day on.

The significance of rote, intentionless prayer is a question that may be examined from the halakhic or general religious perspective. But such prayer can never be *hitbodedut*. The whole aim of this practice is to open the heart. The peak of *hitbodedut* is this (par. 7):

> Until he is very close to having his soul leave him, God forbid, until he almost dies, God forbid, until his soul remains connected to his body only with a thread, as a result of his great pain, yearning, and pining for God. As Chazal said, 'No man's prayer is heard until he takes his soul in the palm of his hand' (Ta'anit 8a).

Rav Nachman once explained the superiority of spontaneous prayer in metaphysical terms (par. 5):

> The prosecuting angels and destroyers know all about the standard formulated prayers, and they lie in wait for them on the roads. Metaphorically, it is like the well-paved road that everyone knows, where murderers and thieves always lie in wait because they have known the road for a long time. But when people go on a new road that no one knows yet, there they don't know where to lie in wait. So it is in our matter, because the conversation that one has with his Maker is a new way and a new prayer which a person says anew from his heart. That is why there are fewer prosecutors lying in wait. But nevertheless, he [Rav Nachman] often cautioned regarding the saying of the other [i.e., standard] prayers as well.

The prayer that occurs in the context of *hitbodedut* is personal and spontaneous, and hence the uniqueness implied in the very term. As I mentioned above, the term also refers to the solitude which is the setting of *hitbodedut*. Why is such a setting necessary? For one thing, solitude is certainly conducive to this type of prayer, giving one the feeling of being alone with the Creator.

Rav Nachman went further, advising prayer in a natural environment, among trees and grass. He said that this suggestion is alluded to in the term *sicha* (conversation-prayer), which is related to the word *siach* (bush). Here is how he explains the effect of such surroundings (par. 27–28):

The winter is a kind of gestation period, when all the grasses and plants are dead.... But when summer comes, it is like a rebirth, and all the grasses wake up and live, and then it is very good and beautiful to go out and pray in the field (*lasuach ba-sadeh*), [as Chazal said,] '*Sicha* is prayer' and entreaties and desire and yearning for God. And then all the bushes of the field yearn, and are included in his prayer.... He [Rav Nachman] said that if only one merited to hear the songs and praises of the grasses, how each and every one sings to God without any self-interest or foreign thought, how beautiful and seemly it is to hear their singing. Therefore it is very good to fear God in their midst, to be alone in the field among the plants of the earth and truly pour out one's prayer before God.

Putting it differently, the psychological undercurrent of *hitbodedut* is yearning for God. Rav Nachman interprets the flowering of the springtime as the arousal of nature to reach out to God. This is the root meaning of all birth, all life. The trees and wild plants are doing what we long to do – discovering their ability to bloom and grow and sing to God, all of which are one and the same. When alone in the field, one's prayer blends with the prayer of nature.

So far, we have examined the parameters of Rav Nachman's program and its theoretical basis. But we have yet to touch on one crucial aspect of this technique – a problematic one. In *hitbodedut*, one aims for prayer as an expression of faith, will, yearning. Lip-service is nowhere near the mark. We are therefore faced with the same problem that came up in the techniques previously studied. How does one arouse earnestness? If I don't have it, can I consciously bring it about? Or to put it more specifically in the context of *hitbodedut*, what do I do when I find myself emotionally incapable of prayer, heart closed and soul dry?

Rav Nachman, as is well known, constantly emphasized that it is forbidden to despair. He offers the following words of encouragement (par. 2):

And even if sometimes his words are stopped up and he cannot open his mouth to speak before Him at all, this itself is very good.

At present we still do not understand what is so good about this situation, or whether there is anything can be done to break out of it. We will deal with this important question, *be-ezrat Hashem*, in the next *shiur*. Doing so will give us a more profound understanding of the dynamic of *hitbodedut*.

## Notes

1. For precision's sake: many of the sayings in this book are by Rav Nachman's foremost disciple, Rav Nossan of Nemirov.

# Shiur fifteen

# Ethical Ascent Through Prayer

## PART II

In THE LAST LESSON, Rav Nachman of Braslav advised us that the road to higher living, morally and spiritually, is *hitbodedut* – prayer offered in an intimate setting in which man is aware of his being alone with the Creator.

Let us continue to study this technique. I would like to open with a question which so far we dealt with only briefly. How, in fact, does *hitbodedut* achieve the goal of ethical ascent? On the face of it, it seems that we have no answer to this, any more than we have an answer to the general question of how prayers are answered. Like all prayer, the effectiveness of *hitbodedut* is part of the mystery and the miracle of God's Providence. But there are other answers that suggest themselves.

One simple idea is that a person who truly entreats God for help in his religious life will automatically tend to take his religion more seriously. An honest person cannot earnestly petition God for assistance if he is not working to improve his situation. But despite the logic in this argument, it does not appear in the Braslav literature I have seen. And in view of Rav Nachman's lack of faith in autonomous human spiritual efforts, I do not think he would subscribe to it.

But there is something else to be said about this. We saw Rav Nachman describe the experience of *hitbodedut* as an intense, perhaps painful spiritual yearning ('until he almost dies'), which requires concentrated, self- transcending effort. Is this effort required merely in the same way that any prayer needs earnestness and sincerity? No, it clearly goes beyond that. It appears that the object of the *hitbodedut* – spiritual change – is to a large extent attained in the context of *hitbodedut* itself. The chemistry of spiritual growth is at work in the very dynamic of pouring out one's striving soul to God.

If this analysis is correct, then so is the following corollary: the possibility of pouring out one's heart in *hitbodedut* is not necessarily within one's power. If God's help is the basis of all religious growth, and heart-felt 'conversation' with God is the vehicle of this longed-for transformation, then God's active help must be sought for meaningful prayer to take place at all. The key to the opening of the heart is not in our hands.

In a way, this seems self-evident. Do I expect to be able to converse with my neighbor whenever I want to? Doesn't he have to agree? Why should my deliberation with God be enabled whenever I so desire? But of course, there is a novel idea here that goes beyond the common-sense perception: *God's* 'cooperation,' His consent to be addressed by me is evidenced in *my* ability to express myself with sincerity and depth.

The truth is that this idea is found well before Rav Nachman, and in fact before the Chasidic movement, in one of the classic works of Halakha. Chazal (Berakhot 31a) quote a *beraita* on the subject of *kavana* (intention) in prayer:

> Our Rabbis taught: He who prays must direct his heart toward Heaven. Abba Shaul says, This is alluded to in the verse 'You will direct their heart, and Your ear will listen' (Tehillim 10).[1]

Rav Yoel Sirkes, in his *Bayit Chadash* commentary on *Tur Orach Chayim* (98), asked: Since the need for *kavana* is mentioned in the verse, why does Abba Shaul call it only an "allusion"? He answers:

> Because the verse implies that a man does not have the power to direct his heart toward heaven, for it says, '*You* will direct their heart,' implying that if You direct their heart, then Your ear will hear, as

Rashi explained. In other words, it is in the hand of God to direct their heart so that they will have *kavana* in prayer, and if not for the help of God, one would not be able to direct one's heart. But at the same time, there is an *allusion* that a man ought to arouse himself and consciously decide to have *kavana*, and then God will certainly help him, because (as Chazal said), 'One who desires to purify himself merits Divine assistance.'

But there is an important difference between this and Rav Nachman. While the *Bayit Chadash* gives us the feeling that Divine assistance is forthcoming as a rule, Rav Nachman is aware of the experience of the help being withheld.

## Breaking Out of Muteness

This is the backdrop for Rav Nachman's treatment of the acute problem that is liable to beset the practitioner of *hitbodedut*. As Rav Nachman instructed, he has set aside a quiet time in a rustic environment, but the words will not come. In the last lesson we read Rav Nachman's consolation: 'This in itself is very good.' Why is it good? And how can we move on from loss of words to discover the ability to address God? Rav Nachman continues (*Hishtapkhut Ha-Nefesh* 2):

> This state of readiness, that he is poised before Him and desires to speak but cannot, this in itself is also very good. And he can make a speech and a prayer out of this in itself; and about this situation in itself he may cry out and beseech God that he is so far gone that he cannot even speak; and he may request from Him mercy[2] and entreaties, that He should have pity on him and open his mouth so that he may express himself in speech before God.

This last is certainly a helpful and insightful bit of advice. But beyond throwing a life-line to the desperately tongue-tied, Rav Nachman says that the state of muteness *in itself* is 'very good.' He is implying that to move from helpless silence to spontaneous speech is not only overcoming a handicap, but a positive contribution that enhances the process of *hitbodedut*. This is understandable in light of what we said above. The capacity to pour out one's heart is a gift from God. When it appears after having been withheld for a time, the *mitboded* is pointedly aware of the Divine assistance. He knows that the prayer itself contains an answer to the prayer. One's yearning for deepening attachment to spirituality is *itself* that deepening attachment.

Rav Nachman spells all this out in the following citation (para. 93), and as we shall see, he actually goes further. First of all, as opposed to the preceding passage wherein Rav Nachman described one whose words are '*sometimes* stopped-up', he now sees a more chronic situation as typical – '*usually* it seems to him that his heart is not with him, and even if he does say something, it is without any feeling of the heart.'

> Therefore one first has to stand like a mute, and only desire and hope and look longingly on high in order that [God] should draw down upon him words as hot as fiery coals…. Before God one must stand poor and impoverished, like a mute who cannot open his mouth, to stand and hope and yearn …until by this very means he merits afterwards to a great arousal, and speaks with the warmth of sanctity, in the way described [in Tehillim, chap. 39], 'I am muted in silence, speechless of good', and afterwards – as a result – 'My heart is hot within me; when I think, it burns with fire, and I speak it with my tongue.'

The state of muteness is itself a silent prayer. The mouth is immobile, but the spirit is turbulent with hope and heartache. The answer to this silent prayer is the ability to pray verbally, the gift of words 'hot as coals.'

Rav Nachman realizes that it is difficult to hold out at length in the state of expectant non-prayer. He addresses this difficulty with the aid of a concept to which he has frequent recourse – namely, that in matters of the spirit, premature haste (*lidchok et ha-sha'a*) can be disastrous.

> Immediately, when a person wants to draw near to God, he must be very careful to avoid reckless overstepping of boundaries and premature haste, God forbid, because this is what causes most set-

backs. It is in the same way that Israel was commanded at the giving of the Torah, 'lest they overstep the boundaries' (Shemot 19:21). But one must be patient and wait long for the salvation of God.... And one must only pray and beseech God a great deal. But in this too one must beware of impatient haste in wanting his request to be granted immediately.... If God gives, He gives, but if not, one must continue to wait and pray.

This principle, now says Rav Nachman, applies not only to patience regarding the *outcome* of prayer, but even to prayer itself.

But even with regard to the words of prayer themselves, one cannot be prematurely hasty, as in the case of anyone who would like that, at the moment he begins *hitbodedut* in order to express himself in speech before God, his mouth will be opened and will immediately speak perfectly, words as hot as fiery coals, and with great arousal. But since not everyone merits this, every time it seems to him that he has nothing to say and no arousal at all, he becomes lax.... Therefore one should know well that this too is premature haste, for it is impossible to draw out perfect speech without the silence and expectation that precedes speech. Because first one has to be still and silent, and only wait and yearn and pine and long for the favor of God, that He grant him perfect speech.

Here Rav Nachman says explicitly that the capability of prayer is God-given, and must be preceded by a period of silent hope and expectation. The state of being at a loss for words or devoid of inner arousal is not a quirk or a chance misfortune, but a necessary preliminary stage.

## Notes

1. I have translated the verse in keeping with *Bayit Chadash*, whom we will presently cite. Most of the exegetes on Tehillim understand that the subject of 'will direct' is not 'You,' but the 'desire' mentioned at the beginning of the verse (not quoted in the beraita): 'The desire of the meek You have heard, Hashem.'
2. This should probably be rendered 'prayers for mercy,' which is a frequent intent of the term *rachamim* when used by Chazal in Tractate Berakhot in the context of prayer.

# Shiur sixteen

# Cognition

Oᴜʀ ᴅɪꜱᴄᴜꜱꜱɪᴏɴ of techniques aimed at self-elevation has stressed the activities of study, prayer and meditation. The working assumption has been that these may positively influence the spirit in a way that translates into a general life-change. I recommend them and believe in their effectiveness, but you can probably detect in this very statement of mine a certain admission. Of course, at this point I don't have to re-emphasize that success in any particular avenue of growth is a function of individual inclination. But beyond this truism, all of the approaches discussed so far have an aura of strangeness about them.

Essentially, each of the methods we have examined is an experiential hiatus, requiring us to suspend our normal routine and to create a window of heightened spiritual sensitivity. When we talk about emotionally attuned study, for example, we are talking about an experience that is a disruption of our normal life-habits. Our emotions as a rule flow naturally, and of themselves. The aim in a session of *limud Musar* is to focus on them and activate them. But the "unnaturalness" of this endeavor is an obstacle to be reckoned with. The problem is two-fold. Firstly, a technique removed from our usual experience requires effort. Secondly, even when we succeed, we may still need to ask – how can we tap a new insight, generated by deliberate attention, and integrate it into the flow of our life's routine?

I have chosen the word "cognition" to describe the realm of activity we are about to enter. I intend this term as a catch-all, a category designed to give a common ground to classic strands in traditional Musar literature, as well as more modern overtones, which I believe illuminate and reinforce one another. The word "cognition" may sound like an abstraction, but what is featured here is *attention* to one's *way of life* in a more immediate way. Once again we are learning a new way of looking at thought: namely, mental *activity*, seen as a form and as a component of activity in general. This lends a different appreciation of the role that spirit can play in the texture of our lives.

In presenting cognition as a distinct and broad approach, I may be in a sense breaking ground. The truth is that as far as I know, the traditional literature does not delineate cognition as a separate 'technique', in the same way that we find explicit directions and suggestions on learning Musar, hitbodedut and meditation. It appears that more modern writers have been the ones to describe and explain this general orientation at length. But it is quite clear that the approach figures prominently in Jewish sources, even if in a less clearly-defined way, as can be seen from the examples that follow.

Our first illustration is a well-known teaching of the Rambam:[1]

One should subjugate all one's mental faculties on the basis of rationality...and always place one goal before one's eyes, namely: the perception of God (may He be extolled and exalted), as far as is humanly possible; that is, to know Him. And one should direct all activities, movements, postures, and all other things, so as to bring about this aim, to the point that not one action be in vain, by which I mean – an action that does not contribute to this purpose...And know that this rank is a very high and difficult one, and that it may be attained only by a few, and that after much training. And if there should happen to be a person who may be so described, namely that he activates all of his mental faculties and places God as their only aim, and does no act great or small, nor utter a word, unless that act or word is conducive to spiritual achievement...and he ponders and calculates each action and movement to see if it will contribute to that goal or does not, and only then will he so act – I consider him no less than a prophet. This is what the exalted One required of us, that this be our aim, when He said: 'And you shall love the Lord your God with all your heart and all your soul and all your might.' This means – with all the parts of your soul, that each part of it must have the same goal, this love…

The goal described is lofty and inspiring (and perhaps too ambitious for most people to use practically on a continuous basis).[2] But our aim is to observe the *type* of guidance the Rambam is giving. The setting is not a sequestered study session or meditation, but life. In this mode, what is prescribed is a *mental activity* – setting up a certain spiritual aim as the goal of everything. This inner spiritual act is seen to be a component of one's general behavior, for it in turn influences outer activity by establishing a criterion – what to do, and from what to desist.

Another instance can be taken from a teacher who was a world away from the Rambam, Rav Nachman of Braslav:[3]

> He said to us several times that he wanted very much that we walk with the Torahs that he revealed. In other words, to walk first for a certain time with a given Torah for about two or three months. This means that all one's service and practice of fear of God should be based on what was said in that Torah. And all one's prayer and speech should be for the aim of achieving what was said in that Torah. So should one conduct oneself for a time, and then go for a time with a different Torah, and so on, until he should finish going with all the Torahs. Fortunate is he that takes this advice.

We see from Rav Nachman's guidance that the approach needn't be restricted to a solitary, life-long endeavor, as it manifests in the Rambam. What it does mean is that for a given period of time, an effort is made to translate a particular ideal into life. One is preoccupied with, and gives priority to, a certain thought. Once the thought is 'there' – in the attentive mind – it may influence life naturally. As Rav Nachman put it, one "goes" with the idea.

When compared with the approaches we studied in previous *shiurim*, it seems that this mental activity is skirting a major issue.

The challenge was always to penetrate the depths of the personality. But in taking the cognitive path, aren't we ignoring this? We raise a thought in our minds, sharpen our awareness of a goal we have set, in order to apply it to our lives in a way so natural as to almost 'let it apply itself'. How does this seemingly superficial behavior work as a means of *tikkun* of the self?

For one thing, bear in mind that one wouldn't necessarily use this approach by itself. One could first ideally study a certain topic and absorb it, placing it at the center of *hitbonenut* or *tefilah*. The main message, charged with personal meaning and challenge, thus becomes a familiar companion. Being 'inspired' by the idea ceases being a metaphor, and approaches the more literal sense of 'breathing' the value as part of one's intimate existence. Once this level of feeling is achieved, the self-identification with the desired aim moves on, and becomes integrated with real life through ongoing cognitive aware-ness. It becomes a force that shapes our view of our surroundings and of ourselves, a guidepost for our daily concerns and aspirations.

On the other hand, it is evident from many sources that this ap-proach to spiritual rectification can be very effective even when ap-plied in its own right, independently of anything else. The purposeful activity, mental and actual, reverberates in the totality of the person. *Sefer Ha-Chinukh* (*mitzva* 16) says succinctly: the heart is pulled along in the wake of action.

In order to get a better idea of what the cognitive method means, we will turn to some other instructive illustrations.

**Meta-cognition**

If I had to select a figure who based his life-style on the use of cognition in *avodat Hashem*, my choice would fall on Rav Alexander Ziskind of Horodno, author of *Yesod V'Shoresh Ha-Avoda*. He considered the internal worship of God – as opposed to the outward aspect – to be the most pivotal (despite his being a Lithuanian!).We could sample his approach by quoting from the book. But in order to get a more vivid picture, I prefer using another document, which is sometimes appended to it. I refer to the author's last testament, which is a kind of spiritual autobiography. Let us view Rav Alexander Ziskind as he grapples with a challenging task – maintaining intention in prayer:

...I made mnemonic signs each time as to how many sacred Names appear (in a given prayer) and I made a mental decision to carefully pronounce each one with *kavanah*. Then by habit it came naturally to think before each passage of prayer, or before each praise, that I must be careful about the number of Names mentioned therein, and then automatically all the other words also were uttered without distraction...

And my beloved sons, let me give you another example from which you can extrapolate further. In the second blessing of *birkat hamazon* there are several expressions of gratitude, most of which are mandated by the sacred Gemara...And one thing is always clear to my mind, my dear sons, and any intelligent person would agree: If someone were to utter a prayer or thanksgiving without any *kavanah* at all, and were to think about something else while saying it, it would be as if he hadn't said that prayer or thanksgiving at all, for "God desires the heart"...Therefore, before I began to say the second blessing of *birkat hamazon* I thought: "There are seven things for which I must thank my Creator in this blessing, each one preceded and followed by a phrase of gratitude." And when I began the first expression (*nodeh l'kha Hashem elokeinu*) I didn't rush to say the following words. Rather I first placed in my heart tremendous rejoicing over God's divinity, and I thought about this great thanksgiving to Him in the course of the words *nodeh l'kha* in order to fulfill the obligation of the thanksgiving at the beginning of the blessing...And after this intention...I mentally counted all seven, one by one, with tremendous concentration...Also in the third blessing, I first thought in my mind that I am obligated to pray in the blessing for five things...

Several things should be noted about this description. One thing that strikes us is that Rav Alexander Ziskind has great control over his thoughts, as well as his emotions. If there is a technique here that can be emulated (as the author apparently believes), it is powerful. Here, as well as in his aforementioned book, he frequently uses the word *atzumah* – tremendous or powerful – to describe the intentions and emotions which he "places" in his heart or mind.

Secondly, it is instructive to note that very usage – "placing" a thought in the mind. This is a recurring phrase characteristic of Rav Alexander Ziskind's writing. The person-subject is treating mind and heart (in effect, the self) as object. This existential stance is indeed necessary for any of the ethical enterprises we have been investigating. Now the focus becomes specifically oriented towards thought-activity. The mind is conceived as an arena of action (cognition), and I decide what will be in that arena. The "I" refers here to another "self" that stands paradoxically "outside" or beyond the self. We are talking about a "meta-self", engaged in a process that can be called "meta-cognition".

Now is the time to become acquainted with an important psychological approach whose name inspired the title of this *shiur* – the cognitive school. The term "meta-cognition" is not my invention either, but a known concept. An enlightening treatment of it may be found in a book in Hebrew by psychology professor (and religious Jew) Shlomo Kaniel, entitled The *Psychology of Control of Cognition*.[4] On the basis of research, Kaniel builds a basic model of mental activity which consists of a "processing area" of thought-awareness, fed by input arising from a variety of stimuli. The area is limited in capacity, hence only some of the potential input will be held in this "place" of conscious awareness. But how does the mind determine what to admit, and from what to bar entry or to immediately discard? Various factors come into play, but of great importance is the "meta-cognition": an "inner eye" with the capacity to oversee the functioning of the thought-process. Equipped with general knowledge about cognitive processes and with perception of individual characteristics, the meta-cognition may judiciously influence, and even determine, what goes on in the mental arena. Kaniel is convinced that "cognitive engineering" of the psyche is an attainable goal, which he hopes to facilitate with his detailed analysis.

I would like to elaborate on one conceptual structure of Kaniel's, because it bears on the ease or difficulty of executing Rav Alexander

Ziskind's continuous feat of "placing thoughts". Many people hold the natural state of the mind to be a stream that flows incessantly with changing imaginings; and hence that "concentration" is by definition a great effort, analogous to damming a river. A person trying to concentrate would be depicted with screwed-up face and furrowed forehead, as he fights off unwanted ruminations and mental rambling. But Dr. Kaniel informs us that we ought to distinguish clearly between *concentration* and *effort,* two concepts which describe the management of mental energy. *Concentration* is a mental force, which *directs* the available mental energy to whatever object has been chosen. We can aid our understanding of this force, and our practical management of it, by picturing it to ourselves. For instance, if we are interested in a very particular task, the needed mental attention may be visualized as a glowing beam. If we are widening our attention, the beam becomes a "ball" of light. If one desires to be in an attentive state regarding the general surroundings, the light-force of concentration illuminates the total environment, as we inwardly picture it. When a person is not paying attention to anything at all, and concentration is not being used, the visualized light-force diffuses and becomes dissipated. Managing concentration, then, can be compared to widening or narrowing a spotlight.

*Effort* is something else: the amount of energy required for the given mental task (maintaining concentration in our case). High concentration and high effort are not necessarily linked. Watching an engrossing, exciting film is a high-concentration activity which may require hardly any effort. The amount of effort needed depends on a variety of factors. One of these is objective difficulty (a tough mathematical problem). Others are more subjective: predisposition, motivation, advance-readiness for the task, familiarity, enjoyment, and anticipated gratification. If so, following Rav Alexander Ziskind's lead may be more feasible than we might initially think. If we identify the ways in which meaningful prayer addresses our inner needs and aspirations, and enrich the action by *paying attention* to these links while praying, then focusing the "beam" may be no more difficult than adjusting the aperture of an optical instrument.[5]

There are practical guidelines espoused by Musar teachers that can be understood in the light of what we have seen. Rabbi Hillel Goldberg refers to one:

> Take any verse that you yourself find moving, said Reb Yisrael (-Salanter). Take it, repeat it. Once, twice, one-hundred times, five-hundred times…A message *penetrates.*[6]

While it may be that constant repetition here acts as a catalyzer of emotion, it can also be understood as a means of "placement" of a thought in the forefront of consciousness. Verbalization facilitates intentional mental activity. It serves "as an external, vocal means of supervision of the stages of internal thinking, which are hard to control and supervise, owing to their inner and rapid nature."[7]

## Novhardok: another look

In our discussion of Novhardok, we described the "sensory effort" which according to *Madregat Ha-Adam* is the central means of withstanding *nisyonot*. Interestingly, other sources indicate that Rav Yosef Horowitz of Novhardok thought that there was one other very important technique, one which does not resort to emotional arousal. This we have on the authority of his eminent disciple, Rav Bentzion Bruk. There are actually two paths to take in overcoming unwanted habits and traits:

> Just as one must implant in his heart and mind the exalted lessons of fear of God, that the heart be impassioned and give one the strength to withstand *nisyonot*, turning from evil and doing good because that is what God commanded; so must one be wise and understanding of sound and true reason, to recognize the good and the bad, until one chooses the good because it is good, and flees evil because it is evil, even if not for the fiat of the Torah.

The first approach involves the building of spiritual strength by consciously arousing passion. But here we are concerned with the second way. This path requires that one intellectually appraise evil as something that one ought to flee, because not to do so is perilous and costly in this-wordly terms. Rav Bruk adduces sayings of Chazal

> that demonstrate the inferiority of this world in and of itself, and that one should not pursue worldly delights even if it were not at the expense of one's *Olam Ha-Ba*. For example: "More property means more anxiety"; "Jealousy, lust and prestige shorten life";…"This world is like drinking salt water: it seems to satisfy but only makes one more thirsty"…Or statements about anger: "An angry person has been possessed by all kinds of Purgatory"; "An angry person forgets what he learned and becomes foolish".

The effect of all this is to develop a thinking habit. By paying attention to such observations of the Rabbis, one consciously appraises anger, for example, as pointless and self-defeating. Once this attitude is assimilated, the temptation to lose control becomes diminutive. These examples illustrate the second approach, which aims to reduce the magnitude of the *nisayon* to the point where the negative trait holds hardly any attraction.

Rav Bruk concludes by saying that where possible, using the second approach is emotionally more economical than the classic "sensory effort" of Novhardok. He recounts that although his mentor, Rav Yosef Horowitz, believed in emotional work as the way to build positive spiritual stature, he also thought that using it in order to rid oneself of bad traits is like using "arrows and bombshells to kill a fly". Educating oneself in certain patterns of thought is in itself effective.

We see that even a school of Musar that held firmly to the importance of *hitpa'alut* had great faith in the potency of the cognitive approach. Similar remarks can be found in the guidance of other eminent Musar personalities.[8]

### *Tikkun Ha-guf*

Another way of looking at thought in the context of bodily activity is evidenced in the following paragraph from the Rambam's *Hilkhot Tefilah*, chapter 5. The Rambam here discusses certain practices which should attend prayer. One of these is *tikun ha-guf*, 'bodily preparation':

> While standing in prayer, one should place his feet side by side, fix his eyes downward as if to see the earth, his heart facing above as though standing in Heaven. And his hands should be clasped, the right on the left, and he should stand like a servant before his master in awe, fear and trembling; and he should not place his hands on his waist.

The Rambam has declared that he is talking about 'bodily preparation'. Yet in fact, he includes here no small measure of inner directives, guidelines for thought and emotion, such as that the "heart face above" (obviously not a physical 'facing'), as well as an existential stance of fear and awe. What does all this have to do with the topic of *'tikkun ha-guf'*?

The answer is that attention to one's posture and movements is part and parcel of attending to one's thoughts. It is for this reason that halakhic authorities have devoted considerable attention to proper physical deportment during prayer. For example, an early code states that "in prayer, one should sway the whole body, as it says 'All my bones shall say, God, who is like unto You?'"[9] In the eighteenth-century, Rav Yaakov Emden[10] recommends some movement of the body during prayer, giving the following instructive observation:

> Such is the way and custom of men of craft and trade, who act deftly and with forthrightness, to move and feel all their limbs, that they be at the ready with enthusiasm and wholeheartedness to carry out their action in concert, fully and truly.

Rav Yaakov Emden indicates that what is true about prayer, is basically valid for all activity. 'Feeling the limbs' – paying attention to one's own *physical* presence as it participates in one's *spiritual* endeavors, is a practical way of arriving at heightened concentration and fuller experience. This connects, among other things, to a research finding that learning is enhanced when preceded by a deliberate 'orienting response' of the physical senses towards the task at hand.[11]

*Rav Elyakim Krumbein*

This understanding sheds light on the preparatory text which is recited before donning the *tallit*, as is found in the daily prayerbook:

> I now wrap my body in the tzitzit, and so may my soul, my 248 limbs and 365 sinews be wrapped in the light of the tzitzit…

Likewise, before putting on the *tefillin*, we refer to God's having commanded us to put the *tefillin*

> on the head opposite the mind, so that the soul in my mind along with my other senses and capacities all become subservient to His worship. And by the influence of the commandment of *tefillin*, may it follow that I should have long life and a holy abundance, and holy thoughts, without any rumination of sin or transgression…

The 'light' of these actions, on the practical level, refers to our awareness of their ability to concretely orient our physical being towards the desired aim. This act of directing is a vital stage in the focusing of our attentiveness.

Here is one more example that may concretize this idea. We are all familiar with the stirring prayer *Nishmat Kol Chai* which is said after the opening Psalms of the morning service on Sabbaths and festivals. Are you among those who are prone to experience an upsurge of intention and emotion while reciting this prayer? The phenomenon may be explained in various ways. It may have to do with the rapturous, poetic tone, or with the the enlarged lettering which the printers usually employ for this passage. I will here draw attention to one feature of the prayer which is connected to our discussion. Consider the following excerpt:

> Were our mouth full of song as the breadth of the sea, and our tongues with melody as its multitude of waves, and our lips with praise as the expanse of Heaven, and our eyes brilliant as the sun, and our arms spread out like the eagles of the sky…we would be insufficient to thank You…
>
> …For every mouth thanks You, and every tongue swears to You, and every knee before You kneels, and every stature before You bows

135

down, and all hearts fear You, and all inner organs sing out to You as it is written "All my bones shall say 'Lord, who is like You?'"

If we think about what we are saying, we realize that every part of our physical being is being summoned here to take part in this great act of song, praise and gratitude. We are praising with our eyes, our arms, our vital organs. This very totality, which leaves no part of us outside its pale, concentrates our attention and our feeling.

When grappling with the perennial problem of *kavannah* in prayer, the foregoing offers a guideline which may be worth experimenting with. We usually try to think about God when praying, which is logical, since in prayer, He is our "Thou". But it is so hard to contemplate Him, because He is unknowable. Will it help if instead of mainly 'looking' for God, we watch *ourselves* pray, try to pay attention to our behavior *as* we stand before God – our speech, our physical position and movements, how we place our hands, the special accessories that surround us such as *tallit* and *tefillin*, the synagogue? It wouldn't hurt to try.

## Notes

1. Introduction to Pirkei Avot, chapter 5.
2. A remark of Rav Yehuda Amital shlita, Rosh Yeshivat Har Etzion.
3. Sichot Ha-Ran, 297. As we saw in shiur 6, the term Torah here is used to mean a specific Hassidic teaching.
4. I will refer here to concepts described in chapters 1 and 3 of Dr. Kaniel's book.
5. In fact, Rav Alexander Ziskind appears to have done just that, as can be seen in this additional quotation from his testament: "My beloved children! All of these practices in service of God come to one as a result of the constantly taking great pride in our Creator, blessed be His name. Let me explain to you the essence of this taking of pride. My heart would constantly burn with unsurpassed joy…that after having created innumerable worlds that tell His greatness and glory, He chose me as well, flesh and blood, a shard of earth, and created me within the holy Israelite nation so that I, too, can see some part of his greatness…and in my heart I would take pride in this, that I merited to praise and give thanks to the Holy One…." According to this description, the intense motivation that pervades the inner life is the result of cultivated attention to the profound personal meaning of avodat Hashem. This makes the task of mental focusing not overly difficult.
6. The Fire Within, the Living Heritage of the Musar Movement, p. 109.

7. Kaniel, op. cit. P. 158.

8. Such as Rav Yechezkel Lewenstein זצ"ל, cited by Rav B. Bamberger in Ginzei Shaarei Tziyon, Bnei Berak 5763, p. 175.

9. Shibbolei Ha-Leket, by R. Zidkiya ha-Rofe, chapter 17.

10. In the introduction to his commentary on the prayerbook Beit Yaakov.

11. Cited in Kaniel, op. cit. p. 75.

# Shiur seventeen

# Summing Up – and Taking It From Here

O UR DISCUSSION of cognition rounds out our survey of techniques and practical approaches to Musar. It goes without saying that the literature has much more to offer than we have indicated here. But I hope we have been able to represent faithfully some key ideas, and to provide a framework in which additional types of guidelines will find a place. Now, in the hope that book has made the goal of ethical and religious advancement seem a bit closer and more attainable, we must prepare to take our leave.

The path we have trodden has been varied. After examining the necessity of actively pursuing Musar, we grappled with the roadblocks that make it so difficult, especially in the present day and age. The ground covered included issues confronting the Musar-oriented individual, such as humility, normality, and religious and secular value systems; as well as questions of methodology, such as matching the text with the person, learning Musar from non-didactic texts, various techniques taught by sages of past generations, which may in turn give rise to additional pathways. Above all, we stressed the conflict between the study and practice of Musar and modern life in all its complexity. I believe that in order to be effective, Musar today must take into account the specific characteristics of the world we live in.

Whatever we have been able to do here is only a beginning, a pointing of the way. More remains to be worked on in order to adapt various aspects of religious ethics to modern life without diluting them. But the best person to do this is you. Perhaps our *shiurim* have given you some directions of thought that can help you develop your own ways of dealing with the problems. In closing I would like to share with you some thoughts about continuing the path of Musar.

It goes without saying that we have not dealt here with all areas of religious concern which pose a challenge to the modern Jew. I wish to mention two of these, in order to suggest that in your future study and Musar-work, they be given due attention. One is *bitachon*, trust in God, along with its cognate concept, *emunah* – faith. Here we again face the quandary of applying an essential spiritual value to a disinclined modern world. After man has seemingly taken control of the laws of Nature and of his daily existence, how does one cultivate the awareness that "the Lord is my shepherd"?

A second area is *talmud Torah*. Torah learning is central to the Jewish religion, and as an action-based precept, is not necessarily connected to Musar. But at various stages of our discussion, we have dwelt on some of the ethical challenges that relate to it. Here is another. If tackled as the intensive commitment it was meant to be, along with the investment of long and regular hours, Torah becomes a part of us, of our characters and our lives. The question then is: existentially speaking, will it be just an intellectual exercise? Of course, the *mitzva* consists in understanding and in intellection. But beyond the *mitzva*, there is the experience. Will the result of our investment be only more knowledge, or also a deeper relationship with God? What about Torah that sensitizes, that engages the heart? These are questions which cannot be simply answered, but I put them forth as an important topic for search and research.

How should one proceed and 'keep going'? As we have indicated previously, regularity – *hatmadah* – is what makes it meaningful. The time devoted to Musar study ought to be divided between two areas. This in the spirit of Rav Yisrael Salanter's division between intellectual study, whose aim is understanding, and a profound engagement whose aim is elevation. The second component is personal and should generally be done privately. The first can be done with a study partner, which is a recommended and time-proven approach to Jewish learning. Rav Kook felt it important that one acquire a broad-ranging acquaintance with the sources, thus amassing useful knowledge and access to different viewpoints.[1] This thought echoes a good deal of the ground we have covered in this book, and I suggest it as a guideline for study undertaken with a *havruta*. For example, one might begin by exploring some thoughtful works of Musar written closer to our time, such as *Shi'urei Da'at* by the Rabbis Bloch, or Rav Dessler's *Mikhtav Me'Eliyahu*,[2] or Rav Wolbe's *Alei Shur*.

## Resources: 'Musar' and 'Non-Musar'

Let us now address the question of resources. In recent years there has been a resurgent interest in this area, attended by publications and a good deal of Musar activity evident on the internet. It follows that Jewish bookstores and the electronic resources are options for the English speaker who is looking for material.[3] I am not in a position to vouch for everything being spread under the 'Musar' label. Serious and good work is being done by people such as Dr. Alan Morinis, an imaginative and inspired teacher of Musar. For specific, personally-suited recommendations, consulting an experienced teacher would be a good idea.

In reviewing the materials on the various relevant web-sites, you will notice that there is a difference between the materials published and used by most modern-day Musar proponents, and the sources to which I have referred in this book. The general trend is to refer to "Musar" in the specific sense, going back to the Musar movement that began in the nineteenth century, and to chiefly study the literature which it generated, along with the previously-written classics which it venerated. These works have figured prominently in our discussions, too. But at the same time, I have tried to broaden the scope of sources that ought to be organically woven into the fabric of Musar. We have used other types of Jewish didactic works, such as are found in Chassidut; works of Jewish thought which are philosophic and non-didactic; and relevant sources which are general in nature, non-traditional and not necessarily Jewish.

What is the theory behind this broadening of the base of sources?

On one hand, it reflects the viewpoint that learning Musar is defined by the motivation of the learner, not by the type of text he is learning. It also hinges on the understanding that the goal of ethical progress must penetrate all the corners of one's existence, including the intellectual pursuits. From this outlook, one can certainly learn Musar not only from the great teachers of Chassidut, but also from modern Orthodox writers such as Dr. Eliezer Berkovits and Dr. Walter Wurzburger. But my argument goes even further.

Of course, one who thrives spiritually on the wisdom of traditional writings alone, need not proceed beyond them when focusing on Musar. But our claim has been that attention to our spiritual obligations is for everyone, regardless of one's horizons, and that this attentiveness needs to embrace the whole expanse of those horizons. It means listening to all the many languages that speak to us, and penetrating all facets of the complex modern mind. Not to do so would mean that there are concerns and interests that remain irrelevant to our spiritual essence – and that is a modern heresy, whose undoing is the goal of Musar.

I encourage you, in your studies and in your work, to do what we have been doing here. On the one hand, cultivate a good knowledge and awareness of sources that are 'close to home' in the Jewish religious sense; see them as 'home', use them to strengthen your basic outlook, respond to their call for commitment. But if in the figurative sense you find yourself spending much of your life 'away from home', where you face a reality that threatens as it challenges, that derides as it dominates – then a serious commitment to spiritual progress means continuing the search even in that 'foreign territory', the general world of ideas. This should be done in a responsible, discerning way. It certainly doesn't mean giving a *hechsher* to all, or even most, of what modernity offers, a good deal of which should be kept at arm's length. That should be abundantly clear from our previous discussions. But what it does mean is that we *relate*: scrutinizing, analyzing, sometimes passing judgment, sometimes distilling, adapting or adopting.

The winds of secularism are destabilizing to us. Exploiting them for good is a way of maintaining our equilibrium. For example, books written by non-Musar writers that touch on Musar-related topics can illuminate spiritual perspectives, by framing them in a context which was unknown to the traditional authors. The modern context and perspective may be the thing which will suddenly make an idea relevant. The realization of such a connection can strike 'home' and be meaningful, even exhilarating. But perhaps the main thing is the over-all effect. The very act of placing the various aspects of our experience in relation to one another, and all in the context of our spiritual quest, serves to make the goal of a consecrated existence just a bit closer.

This recommendation is not without its costs and even its dangers; most Mirrer Yeshiva students should ignore it. But for one who is in any event exposed and connected to the modern scene, whether in fact or as a matter of principle, I would prefer the path outlined above. The dangers and damages to be incurred by detaching whole parts of one's life from the rule and commitment of Torah are greater still.

I cannot resist telling you, in closing, about two things that not long ago underscored for me how dire is the need for attention to this neglected area. In a revealing interview, the director of the Israeli film *Ha-Hesder* (about students in a *yeshivat hesder,* which alternates periods of Talmud study with military service) said that the ideologically saturated environment of the film is merely incidental to the plot. The film is actually about people acting in their own self-interest, which is the way it is in real life, as he sees it. He scrutinizes the position of my mentor, Rav Aharon Lichtenstein *shlita,* that for a yeshiva student, service in the army should express the value of *chesed* and solidarity with the community and nation. Today it is obviously not true, he argues. Yeshiva students that enlist in the elite army units aren't motivated by idealism. They simply want to stand out and 'be somebody'. Rhetoric about high motivation is simply that – rhetoric. Realistically, the idea that someone would excel at his task out of love for his country and people is misguided and wrong. The rabbis who think otherwise are deluding themselves.

Another incident in a similar vein. An Israeli politician of relative prominence is interviewed by a political commentator. A major function of political commentators (in Israel, in any event) is to interpret the entire political arena on the basis of self-interest alone, devoid of principles. The newsman is trying to steer the discussion to power politics, while the interviewee cites his past behavior (i.e., resigning his government ministry over a matter of principle) to prove that he is motivated by the public interest. The journalist doesn't really have a way to refute this, but after the interview he ignores this state of affairs and proceeds on the air with his usual ego-slanted analysis. The commentator knows that this type of analysis is what is expected of him, because it is what the public wants to hear. To the common man, the idea that someone would sacrifice power and prestige simply for the public good is a very real threat – a threat to his outlook and his whole way of life. If such a thing were possible, his conscience would be liable to demand that he, too, be altruistic; that he, too, actualize his self-transcending human potential, his image of God. Cowardice and egotism simply love company.

If there was ever any truth to the position that specific attention to Musar is superfluous, the tenability of such a position is most doubtful in our present situation. Today, a different question – a serious one – challenges us: is Musar possible at all? But we have no choice. There must be a way. The 'way' is something which the sources talk about and help us find. But ultimately and by definition, the discovery can be made only by a seeker. The Torah grants us the responsibility, and the license, to seek. May all of us succeed with the help of God.

### Notes

1. See *Ginzei Re'iyah* p. 103. This idea is stated more succinctly in Rav Kook's letter found in *Igrot Re'iyah,* vol. 1. no. 60.
2. Rav Aryeh Carmel has published an English rendition: Strive for Truth!
3. When using the internet, bear in mind that 'Musar' can also be spelled 'Mussar' (double s).

# Index

**A**

Alexander Ziskind of Horodno, 128–131
Amital, Yehuda, 136t
Amsterdam, Naftali, 86
*Anava, see* Humility and pride

**B**

Bar-Shaul, Elimelekh, 103–105
Barak, Aharon, 60
Bloch, Yosef Leib (Telz), 96–98
Bruk, Bentzion, 132–133

**C**

Chayim of Volozhin, 20, 87, 104
Charlop, Yaakov Moshe, 21–22
Chovot Ha-Levavot, 28–29, 35–36
Conflict
    Inner strife, 42–51
    values, 53–66

**E**

Emden, Yaakov, 134
Etzion, Yitzchak Raphael, 70–71

**F**

Faith, 112–113, 140

Feuerstein, Raphael and Reuven, 72–73
Freud, Sigmund, 71

**G**

*Ga'ava, see* Humility and pride
Guilt, 36–37

**H**

Hirsch, Shimshon Raphael, 11–13
Halakhic man, 15
Hess, Yisrael, 26–27
Heresy, psychology of, 70–71
*Hitbodedut* (Braslav), 110–123
*Hitbonenut*, 83–83, 105
Holocaust, 5
Horowitz, Yosef-Yozl of Novhardok,
    *see Madregat Ha-Adam*
Humility and pride, 25–40
    guilt, 36–37
    self-esteem, 30–37
    self-nullification, 26–28
    Shaul and Amalek, 37–40

**K**

Kaniel, Shlomo, 130–131
*Kedoshim tihyu*, 2

Kook, Avraham Yitzchak
  humility, 29, 20, 32, 33, 34
  inner strife, 46
  prayer, 76
Kurzweil, Zvi, 91

**L**

Lichtenstein, Aharon, 143
Luzzatto, Moshe Chayim, 83, 103
  *Mesilat Yesharim,* 9–11, 84

**M**

*Madregat Ha-Adam*
  cognitive approach, 132–133
  inner harmony, 42–43
  Musar technique, 89–96, 132–133
  *nisyonot* (trials), 42–43, 90–95, 132
Marriage, 55–56
Meditation, 105–108
*Mesilat Yesharim,* 9–11, 84
Methodology of Musar, 7–8, 83–138
  cognition, 125–138
  individual choice, 13, 17–19,
    22–23, 97
  *Madregat Ha-Adam,* 89–96
  prayer, 109–124, 135–136
  R. Yisrael Salanter's technique,
    83–99
  *Shiurei Da'at,* 96–98
  study and resources, 14, 140–142
  *talmud Torah,* 103–104
  'technique' in Musar, 86–89
  thought and meditation, 101–108,
    125–138
  use of texts, 7, 13–15, 17–19, 22–23,
    84–85, 140–142
Metropolitan life, 67–68
Modernity's challenges to Musar, 7,
  142–143
  metropolitan life, 67–68
  self-centeredness, 41–42
  this-wordliness, 10–13
  value conflicts, 53–66

Musar
  definition, 1
  methodology, *see* Methodology of
    Musar
  need for, 1–8
  plurality of approaches, 22, 97
  psychology, *see* Psychology and
    Musar
  *talmud Torah* and, 3–6, 103–104,
    112, 140
  study and resources, 14, 140–142

**N**

Nachman of Braslav
  cognitive approach, 127
  faith, 112–113
  overcoming despair, 44–45
  prayer and *hitbodedut,* 109–124
Netziv, 4–5
Normality and Musar, 41–66
Novhardok, *see Madregat Ha-Adam*

**O**

*Olam Ha-zeh* and *Olam Ha-ba,* 9–25

**P**

Prayer
  Braslav, 109–124
  cognition, 135–136
  *yetzer tov,* 76
Psychology and Musar
  cognition and meta-cognition,
    125–138
  Freud, 72
  heresy, 70–71
  metropolitan life, 67–68
  *yetzer tov,* 69–76

**R**

Rambam (Maimonides), 25–26,
  126–127, 133–134
Ramban (Nachmanides), 2
Roth, Sol, 54

**S**

*Sefer Ha-Chinukh,* 128
Self-esteem, 30–37
*Sha'arei Teshuva* (Rabbenu Yonah), 36
Shalit, Daniel, 61–63
Shaul and Amalek, 37–40
Shneur Zalman of Lyady (*Tanya*),
    17–19, 106
Shopping-mall as metaphor, 61–63
Simmel, Georg, 68–69
Sirkes, Yoel (*Bayit Chadash*), 120–121
Soloveitchik, Joseph B.
    alienation from society, 63–66
    inner struggle, 46–49
    this-worldliness, 15–16

**T**

*Talmud Torah* and Musar, 3–6,
    103–104, 112, 140

'Technique' in Musar, 86–89
    *see also* Methodology of Musar
Teichtal, Yissachar (*Em Ha-Banim
    Semechah*), 5–6

**V**

Values
    conflict, 53–66
    contractual and covenantal, 54–58
    justice, 60
Vilna Gaon, 3–4, 20, 87, 111

**W**

Weinberg, Yechiel Yaakov, 11
Wolbe, Shlomo, 83–86

**Y**

*Yetzer ha-ra,* 56, 112
*Yetzer tov,* 69–76